MIRROR
to the CHURCH

MIRROR
to the CHURCH

Resurrecting Faith
after Genocide in Rwanda

Emmanuel Katongole
with Jonathan Wilson-Hartgrove

ZONDERVAN°

ZONDERVAN.com/
AUTHORTRACKER
follow your favorite authors

We want to hear from you. Please send your comments about this book to us in care of zreview@zondervan.com. Thank you.

ZONDERVAN®

Mirror to the Church
Copyright © 2009 by Emmanuel M. Katongole and Jonathan Wilson-Hartgrove

Requests for information should be addressed to:

Zondervan, *Grand Rapids, Michigan 49530*

Library of Congress Cataloging-in-Publication Data

Katongole, Emmanuel, 1960–
    Mirror to the church : resurrecting faith after genocide in Rwanda / Emmanuel Katongole, with Jonathan Wilson-Hartgrove.
      p. cm.
    Includes bibliographical references.
    ISBN 978-0-310-28489-5 (softcover)
    1. Rwanda – Church history – 20th century. 2. Rwanda – Ethnic relations – History – 20th century. 3. Rwanda – History – Civil War, 1994 – Atrocities. 4. Genocide – Rwanda – History – 20th century. 5. Christian life. I. Wilson-Hartgrove, Jonathan, 1980– II. Title.
    BR1443.R95K38 2009
    276.7571'0829 – dc22   2008033256

Internet addresses (websites, blogs, etc.) and telephone numbers printed in this book are offered as a resource to you. These are not intended in any way to be or imply an endorsement on the part of Zondervan, nor do we vouch for the content of these sites and numbers for the life of this book.

Interior design by Beth Shagene

Printed in the United States of America

---

09 10 11 12 13 14 • 21 20 19 18 17 16 15 14 13 12 11 10 9 8 7 6 5 4 3 2 1

For my mother, Magdalene

Contents

Contents

CHAPTER 1

An Easter Season of Bodies

Bodies, Murambi Genocide Memorial

THIS IS A BOOK ABOUT BODIES.

Anyone who watched the news reports from Rwanda in 1994 will remember the images of bodies. Bodies stacked in open graves. Bodies floating down rivers. Bodies hacked to pieces by machetes. We cannot remember Rwanda in 1994 without talking about bodies.

The movie *Hotel Rwanda* tells the story of Paul Rusesabagina, a hotel manager who sheltered hundreds of Tutsis and moderate Hutus in Rwanda's capital, Kigali. In the movie, Paul leaves the hotel-turned-refuge early one morning to make a supply run before the killers awake to set up their daily roadblocks. Driving along, he stares anxiously into misty fog, trying to stay on the road and get back to the hotel as quickly as possible. But the fog is so dense that as he feels the tires beneath him bumping on uneven ground, he is sure he has driven off the road.

Paul opens the driver's side door to get out and assess the situation. But stepping out of the vehicle, he realizes that he has not driven off of the road. Instead, the road is covered with bodies. It's an image that captures both the tragedy and reality of Rwanda in the spring of 1994.

A book about the Rwandan genocide must be a book about bodies.

But this book cannot just be about the hundreds of thousands of Rwandan bodies that were mutilated in the spring of 1994. Of course, each one of those bodies is precious to God. Each bears the very image of God. But we cannot begin to understand the life and death of these bodies until we consider another body—the body politic.

The genocide of 1994 did not erupt out of nowhere. It has a political history. It happened in a nation called Rwanda, with certain borders and laws and economic policies that had been in place for some time. The killers and the killed in Rwanda were Rwandans—which is to say, they shared a political history where the labels *Hutu* and *Tutsi* meant something, not only about who you were but also about how you were supposed to relate to those who were not like you. When Hutus were told to kill their Tutsi neighbors in 1994, they either did or they were killed. Rwanda's genocide is not just a story about the bodies of some who were victims and others who were killers. It is about the ultimate manifestation of a body politic that was sick from the time it was conceived.

If we are to take seriously the political history that led to 1994, I must also say as a Christian writing to fellow Christians that this is a story about another body—the broken body of Christ. The history of Rwanda's body politic is one undeniably shaped by Christian missions. If ever there was a "Christian nation," Rwanda was it.

If Christians in Rwanda had been slaughtered by non-Christians, it would have been tragic—but perhaps easier to comprehend. However, Christians killed other Christians, often in the same churches where they had worshiped together. Accordingly, this is not a story about something that happened to a strange people in a faraway place. It happened among the body of Christ, of which we are members. Rwanda is a lot closer to Rome and Washington, DC, than most of us care to think.

Ultimately, these three senses of the word *body* help us see that the Rwanda genocide is a story about all of us because it poses a significant question about our bodies. What is the relationship between the mutilated bodies of Rwandans, the body politic, and the broken body of Christ? What is the relationship between my own body, the body politic of the nation to which I belong, and the body of Christ? In the end, these are questions about identity. When I describe myself as black or white, Hutu or Tutsi, Ugandan or Rwandan or American, how is this related to my identity as a Christian? No doubt, these are questions about ultimate allegiance. To whom does my body belong? And to whom do I and my body owe allegiance?

As I have considered prayerfully the genocide that happened in Rwanda in 1994, it has become for me a mirror to the church in the world. But since I live in the West, and this book will be read mostly by Western Christians, the Rwanda genocide poses a particular challenge to Christians in the West. I want to suggest that the crisis of Western Christianity is reflected back to the church in the broken bodies of Rwanda.

Western Christians cannot look into this mirror without coming face-to-face with betrayal, idolatry, and death. So I want to say from the beginning that this is not an easy book to read. But at the same time, I want to insist that this is a hopeful book. I write because I believe in a Lord who took on human flesh—a body—walked among us, suffered the worst kind of mutilation, and then appeared to his disciples again in a resurrected body. I dare to begin with bodies because I have put my hope in Christ.

Indeed, I want to say the only hope for our world after Rwanda's genocide is a new kind of Christian identity for the global body of Christ.

Living in the Midst of Tension

If this is a book about bodies, then I suppose it makes sense to begin with my own body. I was born in Uganda, the son of immigrants from Rwanda. My father was a poor Tutsi in Ruhengeri who grew up working on the homestead of a wealthy Hutu man. One has to know something about the history of this Northern Province of Rwanda to understand how the stereotypical images of Tutsi (as rich) and Hutu (as poor) were reversed in Ruhengeri.

My father was not raised as a Christian. His family, like many Tutsis, resisted the European missionaries. But my father fell in love with one of the daughters of the wealthy Hutu Christian he worked for. He asked if he might marry the girl, and her father asked, "Where will you get the cows to pay for the bride price?" (A bride price is money or goods that a prospective groom pays to the bride's parents in exchange for her hand in marriage.)

My father said he would find a way, so he went to Uganda in the early 1940s and found a job on a coffee plantation. When he had saved enough money, he returned to Rwanda, bought some cows, and presented them to the wealthy Hutu man (who would become my grandfather) as a down payment for his daughter. He promised to return with final payment and left again for Uganda.

While my father was gone the second time, a wealthy young Hutu man brought cows to present my grandfather as a bride price for my mother. Of course, this young man was a much more suitable match for my mother. He was young, rich, a Hutu, and a Christian. So my grandfather found himself in a moral quandary. Should he accept the offer of the rich young Hutu? Or should he honor the down payment of the poor Tutsi young man?

In the midst of this dilemma, my father returned with enough cows to complete the bride price. So my grandfather had to make a decision. He told my father that he could not let him marry his daughter because he was not a Christian. But my father was determined. He said he would go to the local priest and do whatever he had to do to become a Christian. After he was baptized, my grandfather gave in, returned the other young man's cows, and allowed my parents to get married. Then my father took my mother with him to Uganda.

When I was a young boy, I visited Rwanda once with my parents and two of my brothers. But my father died young, when I was only twelve, and we did not travel to Rwanda any more after that. I do not remember my parents talking about being Hutu and Tutsi. To be sure, my family didn't talk much about Rwanda and Rwandan politics. It was, I think, something they preferred to forget. We were not Hutu or Tutsi, but rather we were Rwandans living in Uganda. That by itself made us strange enough.

But we were also a family that took Christianity seriously. I knew from early on that this too could make us strange. If my father initially converted in order to marry my mother, once a Christian he developed the zeal of a true convert. My parents woke us up early each morning to say our prayers, and they took us to church every week, always making sure they introduced us to the priest and other leaders in the parish and encouraging us to become altar servers at mass.

My parents loved to tell us stories of the Christian saints, particularly those of the Ugandan martyrs. When Christian missionaries first arrived in Uganda, they asked the king to allow them to share their message in his land. The king agreed, and some of the first Christian converts were among the young pages who served in the king's court. This caused some tension fairly quickly. Young boys who had put their faith in Jesus stopped making the traditional sacrifices and began refusing the king's sexual advances. The king asked, "Who is king now?" and, with the support of his counsel, decided to reverse his earlier decision and forbid Christianity in his kingdom.

When all of the missionaries were forced to leave Uganda and return to Tanzania, the converted pages decided they could not renounce their new faith. So they defied the king's orders. The king issued an ultimatum. With all the people of his court gathered together, he drew a dividing line and said those who were with him should stand on one side, while those who were going to follow Christ should stand on the other. Whoever wanted to follow Christ would be burned alive, the king announced.

My parents particularly loved to tell me the story of Kizito, a fourteen-year-old boy who told the king it was better to die for his faith in Christ than to deny it. Kizito became the youngest of the Ugandan martyrs. As I listened to my parents tell his story, Kizito became my hero.

Looking back, I realize that I became a priest and a teacher in the church because of the evangelical Catholic faith that my parents passed on to me. But just as I grew up with the tension of being a resident alien, I've also found that my life in the church has been a journey with tensions. Growing up as an immigrant can be a blessing. It teaches you to ask about the history of accepted boundaries and question the assumptions that most people either take for granted or cannot see. It has helped me to see that Christian faith is fundamentally about identity — who we are as embodied people.

In Africa as in America, there is a multitude of powers and stories that try to define who we are: the color of our skin, the nation of our birth, the history of our culture, or the characteristics of our tribe. But when I baptize someone into the church of Jesus Christ, I see that God is making a claim on their bodies. Are they still black? Are they still white? Are they still Rwandan? Are they still American? Perhaps. But there is a real sense in which our identity gets confused (mixed up) with Christ's identity in baptism. Who we are becomes (or at least ought to become) confused and confusing to others.

So who has a claim on our bodies? This is the question Rwanda teaches all of us to ask. If our kings drew a line in the sand and asked whether we were going to follow them or follow Christ, what would we say? After we were finished talking, which side of the line would our bodies be on?

Facing the Contradictions

We cannot look into the mirror of Rwanda without noting its deep contradictions. The slaughter that lasted for a hundred days in the spring of 1994 began on April 7, the Thursday of Easter week. In a country that was over eighty-five percent Christian, almost everyone gathered on Easter Sunday to remember the resurrection of our Lord Jesus Christ.

Just a week before the genocide began, Rwandans celebrated Maundy Thursday. *Maundy* comes from the Latin *maundatum*, which means "command." On the Thursday before Jesus was crucified, Christians remember how he gathered with his disciples in the upper room, washed their feet, shared a meal, and gave them a "new command." Jesus looked at his disciples and said, "Love one another. As I have loved you, so you must love one another. By this everyone will know that you are my disciples, if you love one another" (John 13:34–35).

That is the new commandment Christians remember on Maundy Thursday—the command to love one another, even to the point of laying down our own lives. But one week later in 1994, Christians in Rwanda took up machetes, looked fellow church members in the face, and hacked their bodies to pieces.

It is strange enough to think that the 1994 genocide began during Easter week. But it is yet another contradiction that it happened in Rwanda. If you read Christian mission journals and textbooks from the 1980s, Rwanda is often held up as a model of evangelization in Africa. Nowhere else on the continent was Christianity so well received.

A revival movement spread throughout Rwanda in the latter half of the twentieth century. Church growth was unprecedented. Seminarians in the United States studied Rwanda, asking how they might use similar strategies elsewhere to share the good news of Jesus Christ with those living in darkness. Yet in 1994 an unimaginable darkness descended on Rwanda. The most Christianized country in Africa became the site of its worst genocide.

I want to note a third contradiction for those who have never been to Rwanda. It is an important one to keep before us as we consider the great evil that is possible in God's good creation. Rwanda is a beautiful country—one of the most beautiful countries in Africa. This "land of a thousand hills" is lush with fertile soil, beautiful flora, and breathtaking landscapes. There is a saying in Rwanda that "God travels the world by day, but he rests at night in Rwanda." God makes his home in Rwanda because no other place exhibits so well the glory of his creation.

From my visit to Rwanda as a child, I remember the house of my grandparents, situated on top of a hill. Looking down from the house, I enjoyed a panoramic view of rolling hills, the slopes of which were covered with banana plantations and other crops. In the valley below a river flowed, tracing the curves of a beautiful landscape.

I have been struck by this same intense beauty every time I visit Rwanda. Yet in the midst of such beauty the unimaginable happened. St. Augustine said that evil is like a parasite—it can only exist where there is something good for it to feed on. Where there is greater good, there is also the potential for greater evil. In the midst of Rwanda's extravagant beauty we encounter a story of extreme horror.

Augustine helps me make sense of the peculiar nature of evil, but as I have dwelt on the contradictions of this Easter week of bodies, I find myself asking the question the apostle Paul put to the Galatians: "You foolish Galatians! Who has bewitched you?" (Galatians 3:1). While I trust that there is something to be learned from the scholar in me who wants to tell the story of how the Rwandan genocide came to be, the contradictions we find in this story ultimately lead me to believe there are powers at work beyond the rational progression of history. I cannot explain Rwanda without acknowledging that it has, in some sense, come under a spell.

I don't think this sense of spells is some sort of African animism slipping into my theology. Rather, I believe that Paul is right when he says that "our struggle is not against flesh and blood, but against the rulers, against the authorities, against the powers of this dark world and against the spiritual forces of evil in the heavenly realms" (Ephesians 6:12). We are not called to fight against bodies but against spiritual forces that lay claim to our bodies.

Rwandans are not the only ones susceptible to powers and principalities. When the German theologian Dietrich Bonhoeffer saw Nazism come to power in Germany in the early 1930s, he wrote a letter to his brother asking, "How can one close one's eyes at the fact that the demons themselves have taken over rule of the world, that it is the powers of darkness who have here made an awful conspiracy?"[1] If we say the same when we look at Rwanda in 1994—and I don't see how we can keep from saying something like this—then we have to name and confess the way those powers extend their conspiracy far beyond Rwanda—indeed, how their conspiracy came to include Rwanda through an interwoven history of colonialism and evangelization.

If Rwanda is a mirror to the church, then we must face in it all the contradictions that cloud the global Christian identity. The language of spells can help us talk about the genocide in Rwanda because spells usually remain invisible. This is what makes their hold on us even more dangerous. The first step in confronting the power of spells is to name them.

In the case of Rwanda, I think the words of Cardinal Roger Etchegaray help to rightly name the spell. Cardinal Etchegaray was the president of the Pontifical Council for Justice and Peace from 1984 to 1998. When he visited Rwanda on behalf of the pope in 1994, he asked the assembled church leaders, "Are you saying that the blood of tribalism is deeper than the waters of baptism?" One leader answered, "Yes, it is."[2]

This is the challenge. This is what the Rwandan genocide exposes for the global church to recognize. Christian expression throughout the world has too easily allowed the blood of tribalism to flow deeper than the waters of baptism.

A Pilgrimage of Pain and Hope

For some years now I have been inviting Americans to join me on pilgrimages to Rwanda. From the beginning I always tell them that they will encounter stories of incredible pain. They cannot be overlooked. But still I invite them with excitement because I know from experience that they can also receive the gift of hope on these journeys. Indeed, those who pay attention to the pain tell me they are beginning to understand Christian hope.

More and more Americans are going to Africa these days. Almost every time I fly home to visit family and friends or teach in Uganda, I run into Christians on my flights who are going to do mission work in Africa. These Christians are not just going to tell people about Jesus. They are going to educate people about AIDS, dig wells, teach children, and help start small businesses.

These enthusiastic Christians are doing great work. But sometimes I am troubled by their assumptions. I worry they do not see how Africa's problems are tied up with the problems of the West. But even more, I worry that by operating under the assumption that they are going to "save Africa," they miss the fact that Christian mission is not so much about delivering aid or services as it is about the transformation of identity.

We learn who we are as we walk together in the

way of Jesus. So I want to invite you to come with me on a pilgrimage of pain and hope. A pilgrimage, even though it is a journey to unfamiliar places, is really a journey inward. Every pilgrimage is a journey of introspection. Even as you encounter pain and hope in the places you visit, you are engaging your own pain and hope on a pilgrimage.

As you travel slowly in strange places, the history and geography gradually become familiar. You begin to see connections that you did not see before. As this happens, your own familiar life begins to feel unfamiliar, and your settled identity begins to feel unsettled. The familiar becomes strange and the strange becomes familiar. This confused sense of location and identity can be difficult. Real spiritual struggle is required on a pilgrimage. But the fruit of this labor is a new hope in Christ. Somewhere along the way, you begin to understand that your true Christian identity is as a pilgrim.

This is why I want to invite you on this pilgrimage of pain and hope to Rwanda. I must warn you, the pain of this story is one you may feel in your body. My students have often felt physically ill after listening to these stories. But I want to assure you that it is worthwhile to face the pain — to push into it, even. For I know no greater hope than that which Christ offers us in his body on the other side of crucifixion.

You might think about this journey in three movements: mirror, memory, and mission. While I will not move sequentially from one to the next to the next, these three Ms can serve us well as touch- stones—places to anchor the story of Rwanda as well as our own stories.

I have already explained something of what I mean when I talk about Rwanda as a *mirror* to the church. As we might look in a mirror to see what we look like, Rwanda can help the church in the West see itself more clearly.

But our identities are never simple reflections. All identities are formed over time and shaped by the stories we live into. This is why *memory* is so impor- tant. We can never begin to imagine a new future for ourselves until we find ways to remember ourselves differently.

The church's *mission*, then, is not so much rooted in some future that we've yet to achieve as it is in re- membering God's new creation, which Jesus embodied when he rose from the dead. Our mission is to be a new community that bears witness to the fact that in Christ there is a new identity. It is only by being such a unique people from "every tribe and language and people and nation" (Revelation 5:9) that we can both name and resist the spells that would have us live as tribalized people.

You might say, then, that this is a book about *mirror, memory,* and *mission*. More than anything, though, this is a book about bodies. It is ultimately about learning to embody gospel hope wherever we are.

You don't have to go to Rwanda to make a pilgrimage. The journey begins when we realize God has called us to be a pilgrim people, practicing resurrection wherever we find ourselves. That is, the journey begins when we see that we were made to embody the hope of new creation.

CHAPTER 2

What Happened

Interior of Church at Nyamata

AFTER FINISHING HIS DAY'S WORK IN KIGALI ON APRIL 6, 1994, Father Andre Sibomana walked the fifty yards from his office to his room at the Saint-Paul Pastoral Center. A priest in the Catholic Church and editor of Rwanda's only independent newspaper, Sibomana knew what was happening in his country. And he was worried. He had watched a climate of hatred growing throughout Rwanda, and he had been working overtime for months, trying to tell the truth about human rights abuses. Sibomana didn't know what was going to happen in Rwanda, but he knew things did not look good.

As he got ready for bed that night, Sibomana heard a voice on the radio announcing that President Juvenal Habyarimana's plane had been shot down as it was approaching the Kigali airport. Father Sibomana knew something terrible was about to happen.[1]

The next morning Father Sibomana was eager to

get back to his office and retrieve some important files before they were confiscated. He got up early and tried three times to cross the street to his office. But every time, a sniper's gunfire caused him to retreat back into the church buildings. Finally, he gave up.

By sunrise, refugees were flooding into the Saint-Paul Pastoral Center. They came to the elderly Belgian priest who was director of the Center, Father Leopold Vermeersch, and requested shelter. As Tutsis, they knew they were the target of the militia mobs called *interahamwe* (pronounced *enter-uh-hom-wuh*) that were beginning to gather on streets throughout Rwanda.

Father Vermeersch, however, thought they were simply peasants from the countryside looking for a place to stay and food to eat. A neighboring church, Saint-Famille, usually offered hospitality in situations like this. Father Vermeersch suggested the refugees go next door. But Father Sibomana knew about the snipers already posted outside the church. He insisted the refugees be allowed to stay. Together with another priest, Father Hakizimana, he took on the responsibility of hosting them.

Over at Saint-Famille, refugees also poured in, trusting that the huge brick church building in a highly visible part of the city would be a safe place. Initially, police protected the church, warding off the *interahamwe* and turning away soldiers who came with lists of people they wanted.

But the refugees at Saint-Famille could hear on RTLM radio the same propaganda that was driving the *interahamwe*. "You cockroaches must know you are made of flesh," the broadcaster declared. "We won't let you kill. We will kill you." And that is exactly what happened. Over the next hundred days, some 800,000 Tutsis and moderate Hutus were killed throughout Rwanda—in their homes, at roadblocks, and in churches. They were killed, for the most part, by their neighbors and fellow church members.

I want to draw attention to some characteristics of the Rwandan genocide, all of which highlight an extreme degree of betrayal.[2]

Intimate and Thorough

The Rwandans who killed one another in 1994 were not ancient tribal enemies who had been at odds for generations. They were neighbors who spoke the same language, lived in the same villages—even married one another, as my parents did. How do people who are in almost every way alike learn to see one another as enemies? This is not as simple a question as asking how one brother can kill another. Though tragic, most murders among intimates can be explained by betrayal, rage, envy, or pride. But how do people become convinced that they should kill their neighbors—or spouses, even—not because they have anything against them personally, but because they have been labeled "Tutsi"?

Javan Sebasore, a genocide survivor from the village of Muisozi, tells the story of hiding in a small building beside the church in his village. From his hiding place, he listened as the *interahamwe* slaughtered his neighbors in the nearby church. "The people started shouting out, 'Havyaramanna, son of so and so, you are killing us,'" Sebasore remembers. The victims knew their killers. "They would call out to their killers by name and ask, 'Why do you kill us?'"[3] We must not overlook the intimacy of Rwanda's genocide.

Community Work

Another distinctive characteristic of the Rwandan genocide is the way in which the killing was truly the work of entire communities. We can contrast this, for example, with the concentration camps of the Holocaust. Behind the walls of those camps, SS soldiers carried out the brutal work of killing millions with the modern technology of rifles and gas chambers. Whether their testimony is true or not, German citizens were able to say after World War II, "We didn't know what was happening behind those walls."

But no one could have thought to say that in Rwanda because there were no walls. There were no special soldiers. Every Hutu was required to get involved with the work of killing Tutsis. Whoever would not kill had to be killed. And there was, for the most part, no technology to distance the killer from his victim. Almost all of the 800,000 people who were killed in Rwanda were hacked to death with a machete. People stood in broad daylight, at roadblocks and in churchyards, chopping their neighbors' bodies day after day. The genocide was truly community work.

Rwanda is an efficient and well-organized society, and Rwandans are law-abiding, dutiful, and efficient workers. It is sad to note how all these enviable qualities of a well-organized society were exploited in the efficiency and thoroughness with which the genocide was carried out.

On a visit to Rwanda in 1998, I recall driving through a town where a large tree had just fallen across the road. I was amazed to see how quickly the local leaders mobilized the population for the urgent task of clearing the road. In no time, people gathered around this huge tree, chopped it to pieces, and cleared the road. And so we were on our way again. The community worked with speed and efficiency that would make plant managers at General Motors envious.

And yet I could not help thinking as we drove away how the Hutu Power propagandists had cried out "cut down the tall trees" during the genocide. In little rural villages like the one I had just driven through, the community had come out to do the work of killing together. What force is strong enough to mobilize whole communities for such terrible work?

Church Related

Finally, in Rwanda, as we had never seen anywhere before, churches were intimately associated with the genocide. A man named Adalbert recalls how the Saturday after President Habyarimana's plane crashed—the Saturday of Easter week—he went to his usual choir practice at the church in Kibungo. "We sang hymns in good feeling with our Tutsi compatriots, our voices still blending in chorus," he remembers. But when they returned for mass the next morning, the Tutsis were not there. They had already fled into the bush.

This angered the Hutus in the church, including Adalbert, and they immediately organized to chase after the Tutsi church members. "We left the Lord and our prayers inside to rush home," Adalbert remembers. "We changed from our Sunday best into our workaday clothes, we grabbed clubs and machetes, we went straight off to killing."[4] Brothers and sisters who had sung together the day before were suddenly mortal enemies.

In a number of instances throughout Rwanda, churches became the slaughterhouses. Often Tutsis fled to churches for sanctuary. They hoped that their pursuers, who professed Christianity, would not be so bold as to strike them down in their own houses of worship. How, after all, could you ever worship God again in a place where you killed your neighbor? They hoped too that the church officials and Western missionaries in church compounds would protect them.

It may well have been that when they heard the threats on the radio and saw their neighbors disappear, Tutsis knew that God was their only hope in the world. So they poured into churches. But their pursuers did not relent, their clergy in many cases forsook them, and their God did not spare them from the violence of their brothers and sisters. I have already said that Christians killed Christians in Rwanda, just as they did in the trenches of World War II. But Rwanda is different. Never before have Christians killed one another in the very spaces where they had worshiped together for generations. What makes such a crisis of identity possible? What story is powerful enough to make people forget their baptisms in the very places where they happened?

Once more, we are faced with this question of identity. It is *the* question at the heart of this book. We cannot learn to see the truth about the West in the mirror that is Rwanda until we learn to tell the story of how Rwandans came to see themselves as Hutus and Tutsis.

But we must pay attention to the fact that the enmity between these identities was played out in church buildings. The space Christians had named as holy was not a space that ultimately questioned the logic of the *interahamwe*. Instead, it became a place where they fully obeyed a myth that said Tutsis had to die. What was it about the church in Rwanda that made this possible? As Christians, we cannot look at the Rwandan genocide without wrestling with this question.

The Body of Christ in Rwanda

In 1998 I traveled to Rwanda for my first pilgrimage since the genocide. I went as a priest to visit the churches. I remember on that journey being overwhelmed with pain as I walked into churches that had become memorials—houses of worship turned into tombs.

At Nyarubuye, near the Tanzanian border, we visited the convent church. In that village, one of the town officials had intervened to ask the *interahamwe* if they would be careful not to fire any shots or throw grenades that might damage the beautiful church building. Respecting his request, the killers entered the church, full of people who had sought shelter there, and killed everyone inside by hand. Small children were pounded to death with hammers. Adults were dismembered with machetes. The building was not damaged, but the church was slaughtered. Four years after the massacre, the bodies still lay there as they had fallen, a memorial to the dead.

I remember also visiting the church at Nyamata. In

the late 1950s, after my parents left Rwanda, the Tutsi minority that had been in power in Rwanda was overthrown by a Hutu-led revolution. The new Hutu government exiled many Tutsis into the swampy lowlands around Nyamata. Many say that the Hutus hoped the tsetse fly would kill the Tutsis there. But Tutsis in Nyamata survived, developing the area into a successful trading post. Nyamata became one of the only places in Rwanda where Tutsis had political power. So when news of the genocide began to spread during the second week of April 1994, Tutsis fled to Nyamata. Many of them sought sanctuary in the church.

When I visited Nyamata in 1998, a survivor of the genocide showed me the mass graves behind the church. Some eight thousand bodies were buried there, leaving the church building mostly empty. But at Nyamata, the building had not been spared. It too bore the scars of genocide.

Standing inside the sanctuary, I saw the bullet holes in the walls. I looked up and saw the ceiling was stained with splashes of blood. The baptismal font could no longer hold water, having been partially destroyed by a grenade. Behind the altar, the tabernacle that housed the blessed sacrament had been ripped open. It sat there with a hole in the middle, empty. The body of Christ was presumably crushed, mixed with the dust on the floor. I thought of the eight thousand bodies buried behind the church.

To listen to stories from the church in Rwanda is to enter a history of suffering. It is not a simple history in which the church suffered innocently. Nor is it a story in which the church gets to be the hero. The apostle Paul wrote that whenever one member of the body suffers, we all suffer. Touring the churches of Rwanda, I saw how much we have suffered. We have, no doubt, barely even begun to grieve our pain and loss.

When Father Sibomana fled Kigali, thousands of refugees stayed on the campus of the Saint-Paul Center and in the large Saint-Famille church. The priest in charge of Saint-Famille, Father Wenceslas Munyeshyaka, was friendly with the military and moved among them in civilian clothes rather than his priest's collar. He wore a pistol on his side. When the *interahamwe* and the presidential guard coordinated their efforts and came on April 15 with lists of men they wanted, Father Wenceslas did not question them. He handed over the refugees to be killed. Later someone asked why Wenceslas, a priest, was carrying a pistol. He replied, "Everything has its time. This is the time for a pistol, not a Bible."[5]

Under the World's Watch

It is hard to even imagine some of the horrors that happened in Rwanda. What is perhaps even more difficult to comprehend, however, is that the world watched all of this happening. From the very beginning, the United Nations and news cameras were there, sending out reports to heads of state and the general population. The nightly news in every American home displayed images of the bodies that were being destroyed in Rwanda. But most Americans were more interested in the O. J. Simpson trial in the spring of 1994.

The Bible says sin entered the world through the disobedience of Adam and Eve and that the immediate result in the next generation was one brother killing another. So violence is as old as original sin. But genocide is a modern phenomenon. Technically, genocide is the systematic attempt not simply to defeat and subject, but to *exterminate* an entire people.

While the first genocide in the modern world was the almost complete eradication of Native Americans by European settlers, most scholars agree that the twentieth century saw at least six genocides. From 1904 to 1908, Germans colonialists wiped out the Herero tribe in present-day Namibia, killing some 65,000 people. From 1915 to 1918, the Ottoman Empire killed or deported all Armenians from their territories; as many as 1.5 million people were killed.

The most well-known genocide of the twentieth century is the Jewish Holocaust (or Shoah). Over the course of seven years, from 1938 to 1945, at least six million Jews were killed, along with gypsies, homosexuals, Nazi resisters, and others. Following this horrific period of European history, the world cried "never again" and the UN adopted a Convention on the Prevention and Punishment of the Crime of Genocide. This is when we first started using the term *genocide*. Yet from 1975 to 1979, following the US war in Indochina (Vietnam), two million Cambodians—a full quarter of the country's population—died at the hands of Pol Pot's Khmer Rouge. Beginning in 1992, the Serbian leader Slobodan Milosovic led a genocide against Muslims in Bosnia, resulting in more than 200,000 deaths. And in the spring of 1994, some 800,000 people were slaughtered in Rwanda.

But international observers did not call the killing in Rwanda genocide at first. This is not a term that nation states use lightly. Because the United Nation's Genocide Convention lays out terms and conditions for the prevention and punishment of "genocide," use of the word obligates members of the UN to act. In the spring of 1994, getting involved in Rwanda was the last thing the UN wanted to do.

From the perspective of Major General Romeo Dallaire, commander of the UN peacekeeping mission in Rwanda before and during the genocide, the UN could have stopped the entire massacre before it started. After receiving a tip from an informant inside the Hutu Power movement, General Dallaire sent a memo to UN officials in New York, outlining his plan to raid a warehouse where guns and machetes were being stockpiled weeks before the killings began. New York sent an urgent response, insisting that General Dallaire not carry out his plan. Instead, he was to report the information to the Rwandan president and do nothing more. By the morning of April 7, the stockpiles of weapons had been distributed to *interahamwe* militiamen around Kigali.[6]

Looking back, it is clear that the UN's unwillingness to act had almost everything to do with what they were hearing from Washington, DC. There the memory of "Black Hawk Down" and images of dead US soldiers being dragged through the streets of Mogadishu, Somalia, just six months earlier, sobered officials as they considered the possibility of intervention in another obscure African nation. US interests in Rwanda simply did not seem worth the risk of American soldiers' lives.

Despite the fact that Madeleine Albright, US Ambassador to the UN at that time, was herself a survivor of Nazism, she was not able to muster the moral force to support action by the UN against genocide. Initially, US officials refused to use the word *genocide*, admitting in one press conference that "there are obligations which arise in connection with the use of the term." The incoherence of the American position is clear in this transcript of an interview with Christine Shelley, a State Department spokeswoman, from June 10, 1994, after the majority of Tutsis in Rwanda had already been exterminated:

QUESTION: You say genocide happens when certain acts happen, and you say that those acts have happened in Rwanda. So why can't you say that genocide happened?

Ms. SHELLEY: Because, Alan, there is a reason for the selection of words that we have made, and I have—perhaps I have—I'm not a lawyer. I don't approach this from the international legal and scholarly point of view. We try, best as we can, to accurately reflect a description in particularly addressing that issue. It's—the issue is out there. People have obviously been looking at it.[7]

Indeed, the whole world had been looking at images of dead bodies from Rwanda for over two months. In this case, however, seeing was not believing. Throughout the hundred days of terror in which most of the 800,000 people were massacred in Rwanda, the powers that be in the West refused to call what was happening "genocide." The only direct action Western governments were willing to take in Rwanda was the evacuation of their own citizens.

General Dallaire said that the number of troops sent in to evacuate Westerners would have been enough to stop the genocide. But that was not their mandate. They were sent to save people carrying Western passports and leave those carrying Rwandan identity cards to sort out their own differences. And that is what happened.

Dallaire recalls a patrol during which he observed French soldiers loading Westerners into their vehicles. Hundreds of Rwandans were gathered, watching the white businessmen, NGO staff, and embassy representatives flee for their lives. Dallaire noted how the French soldiers had to push Rwandans back from their vehicles. "A sense of shame overcame me," Dallaire says. "The whites, who had made their money in Rwanda and who had hired so many Rwandans to be their servants and laborers, were now abandoning them. Self-interest and self-preservation ruled."[8]

Dallaire's story helps us see that Rwandans were betrayed by a watching world. It did not make a difference whether Western agents in Africa were embassy officials, NGO staff, businesspeople, or missionaries. They all followed the same logic in the face of the Rwandan genocide. Western missionaries and church agencies, with only one or two exceptions, quickly abandoned Rwanda and left its people to sort out their problems.

I'm troubled by the ease with which this willingness to sacrifice Africa is often covered up by a sentimental humanitarianism. This struck me in a conversation over dinner at a professor's home in Belgium. It was the fall of 1994, after the Tutsi-led RPF (Rwanda Patriotic Front) army of Rwandan exiles had taken Kigali and sent more than a million Hutus fleeing into Zaire. This mass exodus had produced a refugee crisis, and aid organizations were rushing to deliver food, tents, blankets, and other supplies.

Over dinner this particular evening, my colleagues were discussing this "humanitarian crisis." Someone mentioned how irresponsible the RPF government was in refusing humanitarian aid to reach millions of (mostly Hutu) refugees in camps in Zaire. The group discussed this for some time and was clearly offended by the "barbarity" of a government that would not care for hungry people.

Finally, when I could not bear to listen anymore, I pointed out the irony of Western governments who had abandoned Rwandans during the genocide were now falling over themselves to extend humanitarian assistance to the suffering Africans. Needless to say there were some awkward silences during the rest of the dinner that evening—and I was not invited to eat at that house again.

This dinner conversation caused me to realize there is a politics of genocide—and, along with it, a sentimentalism that pervades international relations. In our postcolonial world, Western democracies pride themselves in promoting freedom and justice for the good of all humanity. Indeed, the ideological basis for the United Nations is the Enlightenment conviction that all human beings deserve to be able to meet their basic needs and have their rights protected. The international community often mobilizes humanitarian aid in crisis situations, stating that it is the responsibility of the "haves" to share with the "have-nots" in times of need.

But Rwanda in 1994 exposed how shallow that commitment can be. When Western countries can make themselves feel good about their virtue by offering "relief" to others, they will do it. But when help calls for sacrifice, as it did in 1994, the West seems to prefer sacrificing Africa to putting any of its own resources or people at risk. Despite the rhetoric of all people being equal and deserving the same protection, it seems the lives of a few Westerners were worth more than those of 800,000 Rwandans.

In a collection of stories from Rwanda written after the genocide, journalist Philip Gourevitch tells of meeting an American military intelligence officer in a Kigali bar. Hearing that Gourevitch was interviewing people about the genocide, the officer turned to him and asked, "Do you know what genocide is?"

Gourevitch asked the man to tell him. "A cheese sandwich," he said. "Write it down. Genocide is a cheese sandwich."

Confused, Gourevitch asked the officer to explain. "What does anyone care about a cheese sandwich?" the officer said. "Genocide, genocide, genocide. Cheese sandwich, cheese sandwich, cheese sandwich.... Crimes against humanity? Who's humanity? You? Me? Did you see a crime committed against you? Hey, just a million Rwandans. Did you ever hear about the Genocide Convention?"

Gourevitch told him that he had.

"That convention," the American officer said, "makes a nice wrapping for a cheese sandwich."[9]

Hopeful Interruptions

While this chapter has not been a detailed account of what happened during the genocide of 1994, I do hope it conveys the sense of betrayal Rwandans felt as they were attacked by neighbors and overlooked by the international community. It is crucial for us to remember that Christians in Rwanda were also betrayed by the church. Priests handed over their flocks to be killed. Western Christians abandoned Rwandan Christians again in the name of a higher loyalty that claimed their allegiance.

In the face of these different levels of betrayal, we begin to see the extent to which the blood of tribalism in its many forms runs deeper than the waters of baptism. That is what the Rwanda genocide exposes and puts before us as a mirror.

But the Rwanda genocide also portrays hopeful examples of individuals and communities that were able to resist—even interrupt—the overwhelming betrayal of the genocide. There is a story of a Hutu boy who fled to the bush with Tutsis during the genocide. After two or three weeks, the Tutsis pointed out to him that he was Hutu and so could be saved. He left the marshes and was not attacked.

But this mixed-up boy had spent so much time with Tutsis in his early childhood that he was confused. He didn't know how to draw the "proper" line between the ethnic groups. Afterward when he returned to his village, he did not get involved in the killings. The *interahamwe* did not force him to kill because his mind was, in their words, "clearly overwhelmed." He was a solitary exception to the madness that had become normal.[10]

This mixed-up boy was not only odd; he was a challenge to genocide organizers who depended on a clear sense of Hutu and Tutsi. They could not count on this boy's allegiance to the Hutu cause.

The boy in this story poses a challenge for Christians. Is the church in our time capable of forming people whose identity is confused and confusing? Are we the sort of people whose allegiance cannot be depended upon to further the Hutu, Rwandan, Western, or American cause—whatever these causes might be?

Mixed-up people learn a set of patterns and habits, among them the ability to name the demonic power of tribal loyalty. While many Western Christians can see the truth of this, they immediately think about Africa when they hear "tribe," failing to realize that this is also a spell that binds them.

Westerners do not immediately think of their national allegiances as "tribalism." But that is why the Rwanda genocide serves as a mirror. For Hutu and Tutsi in Rwanda are not the sort of "natural" tribes that we often think they are. People in Rwanda did not just happen to be Hutu or Tutsi. The fact that by 1994 Rwandan society was so neatly formed into identities of Hutu and Tutsi involves a long story of political formation.

The short form of the story is that for many years Hutu and Tutsi in Rwanda lived on the same hills, spoke the same language, shared the same culture, intermarried, and transacted with one another in a variety of complex modalities. Nowhere in Africa, and indeed in many parts of the world, could you find a more homogeneous society than Rwanda. The fact that such a homogeneous society had by 1994 come to be so clearly divided between Hutu and Tutsi "tribes" reveals the extent to which the politics of nations forms us into distinct identities.

In other words, the identities we often assume to be our natural identities are *formed* identities. As we participate in the political and historical processes and institutions of our countries, our identities are formed.

If Christian identity has any chance of subverting or at least resisting the tribal loyalties of our time, Christians will have to recognize the ways in which politics

shapes not only our view of the world and ourselves,
but also the tribal patterns that we so often overlook.

For this claim to sink in, we need to look at Rwanda
more closely and see the story that made both Rwanda
and the 1994 genocide possible.

CHAPTER 3

The Story That Made Rwanda

*Statue of Christ the King in
front of the church at Nyanza*

WE CANNOT THINK ABOUT THE RWANDA GENOCIDE without asking, "How did this happen?" We struggle to make even the grossest tragedies imaginable. In the years since the genocide, many explanations have been offered for why and how this horrendous evil happened. Some have said that economic tensions were pushed to a boiling point by demographic pressure—too many people living on too little land. Others have argued that a "culture of compliance" was easily manipulated by twisted leaders. Still others have proposed theories of mass chaos or demonic possession to explain the unspeakable horrors that were committed in 1994.

There is, perhaps, some truth in each of these explanations. But whatever they tell us about Rwanda, these explanations may reveal even more about how we imagine Africa and ourselves in relationship to it. That is perhaps why no explanation of the genocide has dominated Western accounts more than the one involving "tribes."

I remember listening to BBC Radio during the genocide and hearing commentators talk about the Hutu and Tutsi "tribes." They lamented the fact that "ancient hatreds" had been reignited and "age-old animosities" had led to genocide. Europeans and Americans love to use the language of tribes when talking about Africa. Yet this language is unhelpful in understanding what is going on because it mystifies the reality of Africa.

I am not even sure what a tribe is. Take for instance the Baganda in Central Uganda. They number over six million and possess a distinct language, tradition, and customs. They are called a tribe. But then there are the Walloon in Belgium. They are a group roughly half the size of the Baganda who speak a different language from their Flemish neighbors. Still, they are not considered a tribe.

Does tribe have to do with size? Does it have to do with speaking a different language? Hutu and Tutsi speak the same language in Rwanda. So is tribe a label that is reserved for non-Western people? As a category, "tribe" is very unhelpful, and that is why I suggest that for any Western missionaries thinking about working in Africa, the first thing they have to unlearn is the category of "tribe."

At any rate, to say that Hutu and Tutsi are not tribes is not to deny that these categories are real. Hutus killed

Tutsis in 1994 for no other reason except that the Tutsi were viewed as enemies who had to be eliminated as a final solution to Rwanda's problems. Of course, any of us can argue that these labels did not correspond to reality. But they were as real as the lives of those who were killed. In many cases, they mattered more than a person's life.

The life-and-death reality of seemingly arbitrary tribal identities helps us see the deep influence of social memory and political formation, which is what I want to examine in this chapter. If we will stand before the mirror that is Rwanda, it will show us how we become the people we are because of the stories we tell ourselves.

We are, each of us, functions of how we imagine ourselves and of how others imagine us — and that itself is connected to the stories we tell ourselves and the stories others tell about us. Rwandans became people who were willing to kill one another because of a story they were first told by Europeans and later learned to tell themselves.

This means theirs is not just a story about Rwanda. It is a story rooted in the imagination of Europe, told by European colonialists, retold and deepened over centuries by the church's missionaries, and accepted by converts to the Christian faith. While the story that made Rwanda might be unique in its particularities, its pattern is consistent with the way Christianity functions by and large in the West. Rather than questioning, resisting, and interrupting the formation of identity through racial, economic, and national categories, Christianity so often affirms, intensifies, and radiates these identities. When this happens, Christianity becomes little more than a thin veneer over what we imagine our natural identity to be.

This is why it is both helpful and important to spend time attending to the story of Rwanda. This story confirms that what we assume to be our "natural" identity is in fact the effect of a deep formation that happens through the stories embedded in our social and political institutions.

Land of a Thousand Hills

Despite the assumption of journalists and commentators who imagined the conflict between Hutus and Tutsis to be one more explosion of "age-old animosities," there is no record of systematic political violence between Hutus and Tutsis before 1959. Until the late 1880s, the kingdom of Rwanda was organized (as it had been for centuries) under the leadership of a *mwami*—a king who ruled as the chief authority in political, economic, social, and religious life.

The *mwami* and all of his subjects spoke a single language, Kinyarwanda, and shared common music, dance, food, and stories. We need not have any romantic

53

illusions that this was an ideal society. No doubt it had its share of internal disputes and grappling with other kingdoms for land and power. But the simple fact that it existed without much change over many centuries suggests that it was a stable society.

Within the kingdom of Rwanda there were three groups of people: Hutu, Tutsi, and Twa. Though these groups certainly came to represent an economic hierarchy, their origin was in a basic division of labor.

The *mwami* organized his kingdom under three chiefs: one over the military, one over pastures, and one over agriculture. The military chief could be either a Hutu or a Tutsi. (The Twa, a very small group within the kingdom, rarely held positions of power.) The chief of pasture, however, was usually a Tutsi. And the chief of agriculture was a Hutu. Like Cain and Abel in the biblical creation story, Hutu and Tutsi were brothers who divided the tasks of tilling the earth and tending the livestock. Because cows were the main symbol of wealth in the kingdom of Rwanda, the Tutsi, who were fewer in number, maintained a degree of economic power.

As in any kingdom of this world, this division of labor resulted in the constant negotiation and renegotiation of the Hutus' numerical strength against the Tutsis' economic advantage. Social differences did exist between Hutu and Tutsi, but these were fluid categories denoting more of lineage and class distinctions. Even though Tutsis tended to be wealthier and own cattle, a Hutu could trade produce for cattle and become Tutsi. Likewise, Tutsis could lose cattle or "marry down" and become Hutu.

Clearly, there was a social hierarchy in the pre-colonial kingdom of Rwanda. But this hierarchy did not correspond to any tribal or ethnic hierarchies between Tutsi and Hutu. It was a hierarchy that reflected complex social, political, and economic relations that were negotiated and countered by Rwandans in a constant process of give and take. As I said before, no violence involving Hutus-as-a-group versus Tutsis-as-a-group is recorded in pre-colonial history.

This is the Rwanda that Europeans "discovered" when they came to Africa during their so-called Age of Exploration. It is important to remember that educated Europeans came to Africa with a set of assumptions. They knew (or presumed to know) some things about Africa before they ever set foot on her shores.

Europeans knew these things, for the most part, from their university studies. G.W.F. Hegel, the great synthesizer of German philosophy, taught in his lectures on history that human progress was the result of the Spirit's actualization in history. This process, he said, had reached its peak in nineteenth-century Europe—particularly in Hegel's Germany. German culture was the standard by which all other cultures should be measured. *Advanced* meant "like Germany," whereas *primitive* indicated a divergence from the norms of European life. For Hegel, Africa, with its "primitive" customs and traditions was therefore the "other" of European civilization, the only place the Spirit of rational organization and logical thinking had not touched.

In his lengthy collection of notes and observations about his travels through the interior of Africa, John Hanning Speke offers the chance to see Africa through the eyes of an educated nineteenth-century European. In his journal, Speke not only reiterates Hegel's assumptions about a primitive Africa; he offers a biblical narrative to explain Africa's plight.

A Christian, Speke offered this biblical disclaimer at the beginning of his report: "If the picture be a dark one, we should, when contemplating these sons of Noah, try and carry our mind back to the time when our poor elder brother Ham was cursed by his father, and condemned to be a slave of both Shem and Japheth."[1] In Speke's day, the curse of Ham from the book of Genesis was thought to justify the enslavement of black Africans.[2] But this use of the Bible to explain Africa also reveals how Speke's view of Africa had been shaped in advance by European assumptions—including Hegel's views—about who Africans were.

Speke imagined Africans as a primitive people in need of evangelism and education by Europeans. Wherever Speke encountered Africans who appeared to be somewhat more advanced, he assumed they must be immigrants from somewhere else. "It appears impossible to believe, judging from the physical appearance of the Wahuma, that they can be of any race other than the Semi-Shem-Hamitic ... Christians of the greatest antiquity."[3]

More advanced Africans, Speke reasoned, had to be the descendants of Christians who had come south centuries before. Indeed, he saw in their physical features signs that they were of Abyssinian descent. In keeping with his assumption that nothing good could come out of Africa, Speke attributed what he took to be signs of advanced culture to outside influences.

Along with their philosophy of history, Europeans brought to Africa the idea of race. As we have seen, Hutu and Tutsi existed in pre-colonial Rwanda as roles that determined people's place in society. But Europeans ascribed biblical explanations to these roles, insisting that they could see in Tutsis' physical features that they were descendants of Semites.[4]

The same "science" that was used to justify slavery also measured nose width and calculated average height in order to demonstrate Tutsi superiority. What had been a fluid system of complex relations quickly turned into a set of simplistic racial categories that defined the Tutsi minority as superior and the Hutu majority as inferior. According to the story that the

Europeans told, these two groups were "races" that had always existed. In time, the Tutsi race invaded the land of the Hutu and set up the complex civilization that Speke found in the region.

What must be noted again is that all of this was nothing but European anthropology of the worst kind, which Speke and the Western missionaries after him simply accepted, and to which Christianity now supplied a biblical narrative (Ham) to explain the allegedly racial difference between Hutu and Tutsi.

Christianity and Colonialism

Following the subdivision of Africa among European nations at a conference in Berlin, Germans came to Rwanda in 1897. Though they supported the *mwami*-ship and strengthened its power to govern people in their newly racialized roles, the Germans never had a significant presence in Rwanda. (Fifteen years after the Berlin Conference, there were only ninety-six Europeans in Rwanda, including missionaries.) Though the Germans didn't have time or resources to fully "develop" their colony, their aim from the very beginning was to bring commerce, civilization, and Christianity to Africa. In 1900 the White Fathers, a Catholic missionary order, established their first mission in the country, committing themselves as ambassadors for this cause.

Following World War I, Germany's colonies were redistributed to other European powers, and Rwanda came under the rule of Belgium. This small country in Africa's interior mattered to Belgium, another small country, because of its proximity to the rubber-rich Belgian Congo. The Belgians set out to develop Rwanda into a modern nation state. With the help of the Hamitic story, according to which the Tutsis were the "natural born leaders" and the Hutus were the inferior descendants of Ham, government representatives and missionaries alike committed themselves to transforming Rwanda into a modern, civilized, and efficient state.

I have to confess, they greatly succeeded. As a result, Rwanda is one of few places in Africa where one can see something of the orderliness and efficiency of a modern nation state at work. The country is well organized, the road network highly developed, and government offices generally well run.

Rwandans love bureaucracy and stamps in a way that reminds me so much of Belgium. If you enter Rwanda as a visitor, you are constantly given one form after another to fill out. Each of these forms is passed on to be examined and then stamped by at least two people in the immigration office. The entire process is repeated when you check into a hotel.

Anyone who has been to Belgium will immediately recognize this fascination with bureaucratic efficiency and the endless stamping of reports, documents, and cards. From this point of view, the Belgians succeeded in transforming Rwanda into a mirror image of their well organized, efficient, and modern nation state. This partly explains the success of the genocide. With the well-kept public records and mandatory identity cards, the government through its local officials knew who and where everybody was.

Back to our story. In keeping with their theory of the Tutsis' racial superiority, the Belgians discarded the three-chief system of the *mwami*-ship and said that every chief had to be a Tutsi. In their fixed roles, Hutus were forced to do "communal work" that largely benefited their Tutsi rulers. Meanwhile, European schools were established to educate future leaders. Most of these schools were run by Christian missionaries, but only Tutsi children were invited to hear the good news of Jesus Christ and receive the light of education.

King Musigwa, *mwami* of the Rwandan kingdom, was not very impressed by the Belgians and resisted both modernization and Christianity. In 1931, however, he was successfully deposed by Belgian forces and succeeded by his son, Rudahigwa, who was promptly converted and baptized.

Like Constantine many centuries before him, Rudahigwa led the way in a mass conversion of people who could see that the times were changing. Now decidedly Christian, Rwanda began issuing identity cards in

1933, further solidifying its citizens' identities as Hutu or Tutsi. What had once been a social role and then a racial category was now an essential part of every Rwandan's identity, frozen in time by a piece of paper that told each person who they were.

All of this was thoroughly baptized in 1945 when Rwanda was declared a Christian nation, dedicated to "Christ the King." Of course, this didn't mean that the *mwami* gave up his power—or that the Belgians forfeited any of theirs. Instead, it meant the entire colonial project was given a firm Christian undergirding. The big statue in front of the church of Nyanza where the dedication of Rwanda took place depicts Christ pointing heavenward and bears an inscription: "One Rwanda under one King." The play on words makes it difficult to tell whether "one King" refers to Jesus or the *mwami* of Rwanda.

But the dedication of Rwanda to Christ the King at Nyanza only made public what was going on already. Missionary Christianity in Rwanda found itself part of the larger story of modernization in Rwanda. The church did not write the script but took it for granted and, in fact, found it exhilarating. Church leaders saw their role as one of advancing this modernization project and helping it succeed.

Instead of softening the divisions between Hutu and Tutsi, the church in Rwanda amplified, intensified, and radiated them. But this was not only true of the established Catholic Church. From 1930 onwards, a powerful revival swept through the region and attracted many followers. Significant as this revival was, it never offered any revision of Hutu/Tutsi categories (or Rwanda politics). Instead, the revivalists understood their role as offering the cultural and spiritual translation needed to make modern Rwanda work.

This was brought home to me on a recent visit to Rwanda. I talked with the pastor of a new megachurch outside Kigali. "Rwandans are religiously skeptical but spiritually hungry," he told me—something that I often hear pastors in the United States say about middle-class Americans. This Rwandan pastor spoke with great excitement about President Kagame's "2020 Vision" and the rising middle class in Rwanda. He shared passionately about his desire to make the gospel spiritually and culturally relevant to Rwandans in this new post-genocide era. "Rwandans don't have to walk," he said to me, repeating Kagame's 2020 Vision. "They can run!"

I do not mean to single out this particular pastor. There are others like him in Rwanda—and many more whom I have met and talked with in the United States. I do not doubt the sincerity or the passion of their faith. My worry is about the apparent failure to learn anything from the past—even when that past is as tragic as genocide. Even if that past is not yet fifteen years behind us.

Christians who feel called to get involved in Africa today must take this history seriously. Sincerity and passion are not enough to ensure faithful social engagement. Speke was sincere, and he was nothing if not passionate. Many of the White Fathers were sincere missionaries. But they were caught up in a history they did not understand. Well-educated and pious church members, they became tools of a colonial project to "civilize" and use African people.

We need not single out for blame the individuals who left their homes and families to serve the church in Rwanda. While they were certainly responsible for their actions, they were also part of a larger body—a church that sent them, prayed for them, and enjoyed the benefits of the colonial project. The church that the *mwami* built opposite his palace was a mirror image of the colonialists' churches back home. The same is true today. None of us can stand back and say that we are not implicated where the church has become married to the kingdoms of this world and their desire for "progress."

Turning the Tables

The truth about Rwanda is that the church played a central role in the development of a society where the Tutsi minority ruled a Hutu majority. In time, however, the tables turned, and the church played an important role in this revolution as well. The history of Belgium plays a significant part in the Rwandan story of the twentieth century. In Belgium, the aristocratic French had ruled the Flemish harshly for generations. In the 1950s a Flemish revolt led to a divided Belgium with separate governments and educational systems. With more Flemish priests sensitive to their people's struggle serving as missionaries in Rwanda, the social movement for Hutu liberation was fomented.

Reading their own story onto the situation in Rwanda, Flemish priests sympathized with the oppressed Hutu, who were already beginning to rise up and refuse the injustices that Belgian authorities and their Tutsi clients were committing against them. But the Hutus were not the only ones seeking change. By this time, Tutsis were growing dissatisfied with Belgian rule. King Rudahigwa was meeting with other African leaders and representatives of the UN to discuss independence. Soon he was found dead.

Rudahigwa's assassination created the perfect storm for a "Social Revolution" in which Hutus took over the Rwandan government and ultimately gained independence from Belgian rule. Much of the energy for this revolution came from Catholic priests and the Hutu students they had taught. What followed in 1959 was the first ever large-scale massacre—20,000 Tutsis were killed.

Looking back at the history of Rwanda, it is striking

to see how the church could name the injustice of the colonial system without fundamentally questioning its power to determine who people are. Rwanda's Social Revolution turned the tables by giving power to the majority Hutu and sending many of the Tutsi running for their lives. Some thirty years later, the children of exiled Tutsis would return with the RPF army to defend fellow Tutsis against Hutu Power and ultimately bring the genocide to an end after the hundred days of slaughter.

But in all of this, no one was ever able to say that the racial categories of Hutu and Tutsi were part of the colonialists' propaganda. Rwandans didn't even get rid of their identity cards. Hutu and Tutsi had become so fixed—so natural—that people could not begin to imagine how they might live without these categories.

While visiting a genocide site in Rwanda, I remember seeing a young woman who was scattering lime on the dead bodies to preserve them for viewing at the memorial. I was so disturbed by the sight of her slowly going about her work that I made a point to talk with her. "Does this job give you nightmares?" I asked.

"No," she replied without further comment. She just kept spreading the lime.

"Where were you during the genocide?" I asked.

"I was here."

"Were you afraid?"

"No," she said without emotion. "I was not one of the ones to be killed."

I was struck by how casually this woman named the reality that seemed so natural in Rwanda. She was Hutu. The Hutus were not the ones to be killed. For her, that was the end of the story. She saw no reason to question these identities, no space to ask what the difference was between a Hutu and a Tutsi. This was simply the way things were. The categories could neither be questioned nor changed.

By paying attention to the story that made Rwanda, we begin to see how all nations are made by stories. Often we think that nations are made by the generals who fight wars or the politicians who negotiate settlements or the corporations that broker deals. In the struggle for power, nations often seek more military might, more political influence, or a larger gross national product. All of these factors influence history, of course, but none is as powerful as the stories we tell ourselves about who we are.

The interweaving of European colonialism and the Hamitic myth helped to create modern Rwanda. Just as one cannot understand the Rwanda of 1994 without this story and the social history that it took, one cannot understand any nation and its politics without getting to the heart of the story that shapes that people.

Stories shape not only communities but our very lives. Our identities are shaped by stories that become embedded in the social and political institutions of everyday life. In Rwanda of 1994 we see a community neatly divided between Hutu and Tutsi, in which these identities had become natural, but when you look back at 1890 where we began Rwanda's story, it is clear that these so-called natural identities are formed in and through a history of social political processes and interactions.

So Rwanda's social history reveals to us how stories can kill. Yes, people did the killing in Rwanda. Yes, they needed weapons to do it. But apart from the story that taught Rwandans to understand themselves as Hutu and Tutsi, eternally at odds with one another, the genocide could not have happened. The very same people could just as easily have been neighbors, using their machetes to farm instead of kill.

But once a vision of Hutu and Tutsi as fundamentally different people who must always be at war with one another had become entrenched into the collective imagination of Rwandans, this story could easily be called upon to justify the killing of Tutsis. Over a century-and-a-half after Speke first told the story of Tutsis being foreign invaders from Ethiopia, Hutu extremists were calling on their Hutu compatriots to send the Tutsis back to Ethiopia via the river. Within weeks, the Akagera River was literally flooded with bodies of dead Tutsis.

Once this imagination and identity had fomented,

Christianity made little difference in Rwanda. Christianity seemed little more than an add-on—an inconsequential relish that did not radically affect people's so-called natural identities, nor the goals or purposes they pursued. Purposes and goals were dictated to Christians and non-Christians alike by radio personalities and political figures.

What we are seeing is how the blood of tribalism comes to run deeper than the waters of baptism. This, I suspect, is true not only in Rwanda. The story we have told about Rwanda helps us to see the process through which this happens—the process through which this eventually comes to be accepted as normal. A similar process of narrating is needed if one is to understand the form, shape, and effect the story of inconsequential Christianity takes in different places.

As a pastor and theologian, I am tempted to look at the Rwandan genocide and ask, "How could the church have acted differently?" I want to say what we must do as a church—as human beings, even—to prevent this kind of horrendous evil from happening again. But that Hutu woman in the churchyard reminds me that our deepest problem is a poverty of imagination.

We do not need someone to tell us what to do as much as we need someone to help us imagine new possibilities. Could the story of Rwandan Christianity have been different? How so? What imaginative possibilities could the church have offered Rwandans beyond the labels of Hutu and Tutsi?

The story that made Rwanda teaches us how much we need the renewal of our minds that the gospel promises.

Renewing the Christian Mind

This is how the apostle Paul articulated Jesus' call to repentance: "Do not conform to the pattern of this world, but be transformed by the renewing of your mind" (Romans 12:2). Paul goes on to say that we must present our bodies as a living sacrifice. (We'll talk more about bodies and the pattern of this world in the next chapter.)

But before we can start serving God with our bodies, our minds must change. They have to be made new, says Paul. Again, our deepest problem is our poverty of imagination. So our transformation must begin with the renewal of our minds. And that is what the Christian story is about—offering a fresh lens through which to see ourselves, others, and the world. In the process, Christianity is meant to shape a new identity within us by creating a new sense of *we*—a new community that defies our usual categories of anthropology.

Jesus was born into a story that said Jews were the legitimate heirs of Abraham and Samaritans were an inferior mixed breed. Those were the accepted categories of his day. In the fourth chapter of John's gospel, Jesus led his disciples into "enemy" territory to question those categories head-on.

"Now he had to go through Samaria," John tells us. Driven by fear, many Jews in Jesus' day made a point to walk around Samaria, not through it. But Jesus takes the most direct route, walking through the homeland of a people who are supposed to be his enemies.

As it happens when people take a long journey in a hot and dry region, Jesus grew tired and thirsty. Seeing a well, he sat down beside it to rest. When a Samaritan woman came to draw water, Jesus asked her, "Will you give me a drink?" (John 4:7). I can't help but notice the weakness of Jesus' position. He is worn out from his journey, in desperate need of water. His throat is parched and he can only muster a few words: "Will you give me a drink?"

It is almost as if Jesus has forgotten that he is in enemy territory, as he asks a lowly Samaritan woman for help. The woman, however, does not forget the story that has shaped her people. "You are a Jew and I am a Samaritan woman," she says to him. "How can you ask me for a drink?" (4:9). How could this man be so naive as to completely ignore the political identities that were vitally important to everyone in their day? Did he not remember that he was a Jew and she a Samaritan? Didn't he know that Jews did not speak to Samaritans—much less ask them for help?

Evidently Jesus did not know. His mind was not held captive by the story that made Jews and Samaritans into peoples at odds with one another.

"Believe me ...," Jesus eventually said to this Samaritan woman, "a time is coming and has now come when the true worshipers will worship the Father in the Spirit and in truth, for they are the kind of worshipers the Father seeks" (4:21a, 23). Jesus knew a different story about who we are and what we were made for. He spoke to the Samaritan woman—as he speaks to each of us—about a Father who loves us.

We are, each of us, created to worship our true Father in spirit and in truth. As Paul said to the Romans, we are called to offer up our bodies "as a living sacrifice, holy and pleasing to God—this is true worship" (Romans 12:1). As we inhabit the mind of Christ, we learn to see the world anew. Free from the stories that held us captive, we forget the categories that used to be so certain in our minds. We learn to question easy assumptions about tribe, race, ethnicity, and nation.

The renewal of our minds is absolutely crucial if we are to worship God in spirit and in truth. Such renewal requires what I call "anthropological naivety."

This is what missionary Christianity in Rwanda lacked. The missionaries knew far too much about Africa before they set foot in Rwanda. They already had in their minds all those categories of race and tribe, primitive and advanced. As a result, they could not allow for a new Christian social reality that would not follow the logic of race, modernity, and so-called Western civilization.

The real problem was that the missionaries' view of Christianity was wedded to the story of their nations. This is still true in many cases. When Western Christians go to Africa, they already know too much. This is how it has been since the very beginning of missions in Africa. You might say that Western Christianity is overeducated in a story that holds their minds captive.

We can only begin to repent, then, by looking at Africa again with a certain naiveté. We must ask how to see Africa in a fresh way. How can we see through the story that shapes us by knowing African brothers and sisters in light of a different story?

The renewal of our minds is absolutely crucial if we are to worship God in spirit and truth. But the renewal of our minds is not enough, because worship is work that we do with our bodies—and our bodies, like our minds, have been shaped by the stories we live by.

That is why before we can begin to imagine the new reality into which Jesus invites us, we need to take a closer look at the stories that shape our bodies in the world.

CHAPTER 4

The Stories That Form Us

Capitol Hill, Washington, DC

BEING AN OUTSIDER CAN BE A BLESSING. EVERY MORNING when I wake up in the United States, I'm reminded that I'm not supposed to be here. Why am I, a Ugandan, living in North Carolina? How am I, a Catholic priest, teaching at a Protestant seminary? I am a resident alien—an outsider trying to make sense of the way things work in this world and how I fit into it.

Because I do not fit the patterns of this country, I can never take America (or Duke University, where I teach) for granted. I constantly find myself negotiating its challenges and demands even as it tries to mold me into its patterns. At any rate, being an outsider living on the inside has led me to attend more carefully to the stories that shape the lives and identities of Christians in America.

In the last chapter we looked closely at the story that shaped Rwanda, noting how the colonialist imagination captivated the minds of Rwandans, convincing them that they were and always had been two distinct races called Hutu and Tutsi. What I tried to suggest at the end of the chapter was that Rwanda's story is not unlike the stories that shape Christians in the West. Beginning with our poverty of imagination, we start to see how our whole lives can be held captive by the pattern of this world.

But this is not an easy thing to get our heads around. We are too deeply shaped by this pattern to see the tragedy of Rwanda's history and immediately say, "We will not let that happen to us." The truth is that stories get embodied and become institutionalized in our world. They are not just ideas in our heads or words in the air. They are written into our education and health care, daily shopping and common meals. To look into the mirror that is Rwanda, we need to pay closer attention to how our identities get shaped by stories that so often remain hidden.

Naming the Silences

One reason we are unable to see the stories that shape us is that we are afraid that thinking about our lives this way takes away our personal responsibility. It may seem like the story I have told blames the Belgians for what happened in 1994, thereby letting the instigators of the genocide off the hook. But that is not my point. We do not tell stories in order to assign blame.

The point of Genesis 3 is not to blame Adam and Eve for original sin so the rest of us are free not to worry about the sins we commit. It is, rather, to help us see our own lives, desires, and temptations reflected in the story of Adam and Eve. In the same way, we do not seek to understand the pattern of this world so we can blame someone else for the mess we're in. We need to know how to name this pattern so we can recognize God's alternative and live into it.

In short, understanding how we are shaped does not give us an excuse for sin. Instead, it helps us name the spells whose invisible power holds us in bondage, unable to see and pursue the better alternatives God sets before us.

But how do we begin to see the stories that have shaped us? And how can Rwanda help clarify our vision? I suspect that even after reading the story I have told about Rwanda, many will still find it difficult to see the pattern of identity formation that is going on with Christians in the West. Perhaps another way to make the bridge is to note at least two silences that we must overcome if we are to honestly look into the mirror that is the story of Rwanda.

The first is a silence about history. Though we rarely come out and say it, it is striking how often we assume that tragedies like the Rwanda genocide "just happened." Very few journalists in 1994 tried to narrate a series of events that led up to the genocide. At most, they went back to 1990, when the Tutsi RPF army crossed the Ugandan border and invaded Rwanda.

Without the history that we examined in the last chapter, assessments of the situation easily turned into a blame game between warring parties. But there was a great silence in all of those debates that seemed to assume the 1994 genocide came out of nowhere. The same is true for us. As we seek to understand the stories that shape us, it is important to name the silence of history in so many of the stories we tell. Gang violence didn't "just happen" in US cities. The war on terror didn't *just happen*. There is a history that we have to account for. When we don't, it is easy to assume that things such as tribe, race, and terrorism are natural, or simply the way things are.

There is another silence I want to name: the silence of geography. Almost anyone who talks about the Rwandan genocide in the West assumes that it was an isolated event. It happened *over there*. It happened in a place completely unlike the ones we know. This is the silence of geography.

I encounter a silence of geography when the news account of a murder that happened in the West End neighborhood of Durham, North Carolina, is told. I am taught to breathe a sigh of relief because the West End is *over there*. The West End is not so far away, though; I drive through it every day to get to my office. Many of the people who sweep the floors in our seminary live in the West End. How is it, then, that the West End seems as far away as Rwanda?

When we overcome these silences of history and of geography and look honestly at the story of genocide in Rwanda, we begin to realize that Rwanda is not as far away as we might imagine. In truth, the story of Rwanda reflects the same patterns of identity formation that are found in the West. Perhaps one way to make this point stick is through a thought experiment. Let's call it a modern parable.

Imagine that the year is 2002. Extraterrestrial forces descend on Capitol Hill with powers previously unknown to humankind. Not knowing any of the history of US politics, these ETs—let's call them *Muzungus*—notice that the people on Capitol Hill are divided into two groups, Republicans and Democrats. The Republicans, they can see, are in control. They meet in committees, write long documents about how their society will be organized, and then push these bills through Congress and into law. These Republicans seem to be shrewd, capable, and effective leaders. Democrats, on the other hand, seem scattered and ineffective. They make arguments against the Republicans in the newspapers and in debates, but they never win.

Now, imagine that a Muzungu who is part of this invasion sits down to write in his journal about Republicans and Democrats. He observes these general differences between the two groups and tries to explain them. The Democrats, he notes, are generally smaller. They have less money and appear to be intellectually inferior. (There are exceptions, of course, but he thinks they only prove the rule.) Republicans, on the other hand, are natural-born leaders. They are good in business and strong in national security. Our Muzungu explorer records all of this in his journal, carries it back to his home planet, and publishes his eyewitness report of the people in this newly discovered land.

Imagine that the Muzungus, realizing their superior strength and the resources available on planet earth, decide to take over the United States. Rather than relocate a large number of their population to earth, the Muzungus decide to cultivate a good relationship with the "naturally superior" Republicans and put them in charge of things. They give Muzungu technology to the Republicans and help them write laws excluding Democrats from leadership. They set up schools for young Republicans and even give some of them opportunities to travel to planet Muzungu and get further education. They take land from Democrats who, it is simply assumed, do not know how to manage it anyway — and give it to Republicans instead. In short, they develop an entire set of social institutions that assume Republicans are not only superior but also essentially different from Democrats.

If you can imagine such an outlandish scenario, then ask yourself, what might America look like fifty years after this Muzungu invasion? What would happen to Democrats if they had little or no economic power, no access to education, and no opportunity to lead? How would Republicans imagine themselves if they grew up in a society that assumed they were naturally superior to Democrats?

As unlikely as this story may sound, can you imagine what the world would look like to people who grew up in a context where something much like this story was the official history taught in public schools?

Obviously, this is a thought experiment that invites us to consider what it means to be a Rwandan. But the story that made Rwanda was a story from somewhere else; it was imposed from outside. It was a story told by outsiders who were already living its assumptions in their journeys of exploration and discovery. So the point is not just to imagine what it would be like to be a Rwandan. The point is to try to see how, like the extraterrestrial Muzungus, Westerners are shaped by stories that tell them not only who Africans are, but also who they are. These stories are so completely institutionalized that we almost never hear them. They are almost always taken for granted.

For instance, many Americans participate in the political processes without ever stopping to consider the story behind this American democracy. We all marvel at how the American political system works, setting up rules and procedures, dictating guidelines for voting and the separation of powers, declaring national and public holidays, and so on.

Americans sing the national anthem, salute the flag, and pay taxes without much thought. These things are taken for granted. But this system did not just appear out of nowhere. Its starting point (and its justification) is always connected to a story—a story like the one told by Thomas Hobbes in *Leviathan*. In his classic work of political theory, Hobbes imagined human beings in a "state of nature," each living independently of everyone else, acting only in his or her own self-interest, without regard for others. This self-interest led to what Hobbes called the "state of war," a way of life that is certain to prove "solitary, poor, nasty, brutish, and short."[1]

The only escape for humans, Hobbes imagined, was to enter into contracts—mutually beneficial agreements that surrender our individual interests in order to achieve the advantages of security that only a social existence can provide. That is the basis of sovereignty invested in one absolute leader or "Leviathan."

What is significant in Thomas Hobbes's story is not only the assumption that human beings are driven by self-interest and united only by mutual contract. His story also assumes that the only relationship between those who belong to one sovereignty and those who do not, is that of a state of war.

To the extent that Hobbes's assumptions frame the

social and political institutions of the West, they have
come to be self-fulfilling. This story forms people who
are indeed self-interested and who always imagine between their sovereignty and that of others a permanent
"war of nature."

This is why nations find it no problem at all to mobilize their citizens to war to defend their national interests. It does not matter whether these citizens are
Christians or not, or whether in so doing they will
be killing other Christians. The story of national sovereignty runs far deeper than any bonds that Christians in one country share with Christians of another
country.

The formation of a national identity so strong that
Christians are willing to kill other Christians is the
effect of a powerful story that has come to be institutionalized in a country's social and political structures.
Over time, we've given it the authority of being "just
the way things are."

Consider, for a moment, how this holds true for our
economic institutions. We wake up, go shopping, in-
vest in the stock market, buy and sell, make transac-
tions, seek jobs, and exchange services. In a word, we
participate in the economy. But this capitalist economy
did not just show up. It started somewhere.

Connected to this beginning (and always justify-
ing it) is a story—like the one told by Adam Smith in
The Wealth of Nations. Many people have never heard

of Adam Smith, but without the story he told us, it would be difficult—if not impossible—to understand modern capitalist economy.

In the beginning, Smith said, everyone was in competition with one another for limited resources. Like trees in the forest, they competed to grow toward the light and not die in another tree's shadow. This meant that the strongest and best survived through a natural process, thus producing the best society possible. There was no need to correct for economic injustices, Smith said. An "invisible hand," like Mother Nature, would take care of that. Each person simply needed to do his or her best to climb toward the light in order to achieve the best possible human society.

Because the stories of Hobbes and Smith are thoroughly institutionalized in the politics of modern nation states and economies of capitalist societies, we hardly ever have to tell them. Yet their basic assumptions shape almost everything we do in the modern world. Notice, for example, how Hobbes's story assumes that without the contracts of modern politics, we would slip back into the original human chaos of all-against-all. We need nation states, this story tells us. Indeed, we need them so much that we will kill and even die for them.

Notice also how both stories assume that we are naturally self-interested individuals who have to figure out how to live together in this world. Neither story pauses to question what the Bible calls greed. As a matter of fact, Smith says greed is ultimately good for society.

When we probe the foundational stories of Western society, their assumptions seem to be quite anti-Christian. Yet these are not just the assumptions of a story *out there*. This story is written on all of our hearts. The story that makes the West is very much the "pattern of this world" (Romans 12:2) that binds us. Failing to see it, we live our lives according to its script.

A story that assumes we are selfish and self-interested people gives rise to institutions based on that assumption. These institutions of society in turn form us into selfish and self-interested people. As we participate in economic institutions that assume the starting point of self-interest, our purpose in life easily becomes accumulation. The more stuff we get, the more we want to accumulate. This does not mean we become happier people, contrary to the promises of the commercials. It just means we become more aggressive, selfish, driven competitors with scarcity written all over our faces.

Christianity without Consequence

Maybe the deepest tragedy of the Rwandan genocide is that Christianity didn't seem to make any difference. Rwandans performed a script that had shaped them more deeply than the biblical story had. Behind the silences of genocide, Hutus and Tutsis alike were shaped by a story that held their imaginations captive.

. Paying attention to history helps us to see that this was not just Rwanda's problem. The story that made Rwanda is the story of the West. When we look at Rwanda as a mirror to the church, it helps us realize what little consequence the biblical story has on the way Christians live their lives in the West. As Christians, we cannot remember the Rwandan genocide without admitting that the gospel did not seem to have a real impact on most Rwandans' lives. Seeing this, we have to ask: does Christianity make any real difference in the West?

The question is not so much whether Jesus' message has been proclaimed in all the earth. The real question is, what difference has the gospel made in people's lives?

I never cease to be surprised when I visit a supermarket here in the United States. It is an incredible experience for me. Here, like almost anywhere in the world, people eat bread. If I need some bread here in the United States, I go to the supermarket. After I walk through glass doors that open for me, I follow the signs to a bread aisle and face an onslaught of options: white bread, whole wheat bread, honey wheat bread, pita bread, potato bread, tortillas, English muffins—just to name a few. And for each type of bread, there are five competing brands. Could they really be that different? How do I know which bread is best for me? Before I came to the supermarket, I just thought I needed some bread.

On the way to the bread aisle, I pass the meat display. It stretches across the entire back side of the supermarket. Wrapped in plastic and neatly displayed are hundreds of pounds of beef and chicken, pork, and turkey.

I was confused the first time I saw this ostentatious presentation of meats. How could they possibly sell all that meat before it goes bad? Some years later I became friends with a man who worked in a meat-packing plant. I asked him this question that had been plaguing my mind: what do you do with the meat that doesn't sell in supermarkets? Some of the beef is ground into hamburger, he told me. But he said there's always some that goes bad before it's sold. That meat gets burned.

Supermarkets have become a sign to me of extreme abundance that Americans take for granted. It is just natural, we assume, to go to the store, choose the bread we want, find meat at a good price, pay at the register, and go home. No one questions whether we really need so many options on the bread aisle. No one asks whether there's something wrong with maintaining such an expansive meat display and burning what goes bad when 14,000 children under the age of five die every day from hunger.[2]

We assume that supermarkets are just the way

things are in America. Which means we also assume that scandalous gaps between rich and poor are just the way things are. As someone who has watched friends and family members die from a lack of resources, I'm deeply troubled by these assumptions.

But they do make sense to me. Knowing the story of economics in the West, I can understand how people assume that radical disparities are natural—even good—in the evolution of human society. (It is easy to believe in the survival of the fittest when you are born economically "fit.")

What I cannot understand or accept as a Christian minister is the fact that the church rarely offers a different story. I refuse to accept the assumption that all Christianity has to offer is insight about how to secure and enjoy the "blessings" of our global economy. Yes, Christians continue to read the Bible and preach the gospel in the West. But prayer, Bible study, and Christian language easily become a gloss for people who are most decidedly shaped by something else. It's too easy for Christianity to have no consequence in our world.

Consider, for example, how race continues to shape our understanding of who people are. When I first came to Durham, locals were always asking me if I was serving as a priest at Holy Cross Parish. I wasn't, but I just assumed a few people had heard a false rumor or remembered incorrectly a news update from the diocesan paper.

When people kept asking me the same question, I decided to find out about Holy Cross Parish. It turns out that this is the historically African-American parish in Durham. When Christians in Durham see my dark skin and learn that I am Catholic, they assume I am a member of Holy Cross Parish. It only seems natural.

In the US military no one can assume that a black soldier is of low rank, because the legal authorities in the United States integrated the rest of society forty years ago. But American Christianity is so tribal that it continues to assume black people will "stay in their place" and not worship with their white or Latino brothers and sisters.

It is deeply ironic to me that most Western Christians blame the Rwandan genocide on tribalism while taking for granted the tribal divisions of their own churches, as if they are simply natural. A story about natives and settlers, it seems, means more to Christians than a story about the kingdoms of this world and the kingdom of our God.

Christianity without consequence is a problem that Rwandans and Westerners share. I do not write to point the finger at American Christians or to say, as so many have in the post-colonial literature, that Africa should give up on Christianity. I believe that Jesus is the only hope—for the whole world.

But if we are truly to put our faith in Jesus and

the story Scripture tells, we must begin to question the ways that Christianity has been shaped by stories that are not true. I know it may sound naive, but I believe we have to start asking simple questions like why do we need so many kinds of bread, and why does an African priest need to serve in an African-American parish? We have to let the story of God's people interrogate and challenge our assumptions about what is "normal" in our world.

It must be said clearly: the church has learned and practiced ways of reading Scripture and worshiping God that prevent the gospel from making a difference in our lives. Because I believe this miseducation has malformed our minds and bodies, in the next chapter I want to explore three "postures" of Christianity-without-consequence. We need to understand where and how our ways of reading Scripture are held captive by the pattern of this world if we are to experience the freedom of another way. (Otherwise, we may simply reposition ourselves into another of the inconsequential postures we already know so well.)

But it is not enough to understand the problem. We must learn a posture that allows us to hear the good news of Jesus and believe it in this world. After analyzing the prevailing postures of Christian social engagement in the next chapter, the rest of this book is about learning a new posture. I want to show you a biblical example of what it looks like. Then I want to consider what has to change for Christians to re-posture ourselves after the Rwandan genocide. Ulti-mately, I believe this is about learning to stand up by the power of God. It is about God resurrecting the church of Jesus Christ in our world. I believe this is happening. For those with eyes to see, there are signs of something new.

Before we can see it, though, we need to pay at-tention to three postures of Christianity-without-consequence.

CHAPTER 5

Postures of Christian
Social Engagement

Children at church school

I HAVE NOTED THAT THE FAILURE OF THE CHURCH IN Rwanda—both before and during the genocide—was made possible, in part, because the church located itself neatly within the dominant story of Rwanda. Having done so, it was unable to question (let alone provide any bulwark against) the demonic formation of Hutu-Tutsi tribalism. In this way, Rwanda serves as a good mirror to any Christian nation in our time. That America is such a Christian nation is not only obvious in the role that Christianity plays in American public life, but also in the significance of the American church to world missions.

Recently, I heard a wise commentator on American Christianity confess, "We have over-evangelized the world too lightly."[1] In the past century, no church has sent more people to proclaim the gospel and do good works in Jesus' name than the church in America. Advances in technology and access to resources have al-

lowed a multitude of Western Christians to literally
"go and make disciples of all nations" (Matthew 28:19).
Even small churches in rural North Carolina now reg-
ularly send mission teams to Africa, Asia, and Latin
America. But when we stop to look in the mirror that
is Rwanda, we have to confess that this commentator is
right: much of what has gone out in the name of Christianity is evangelism-lite.

Or to say it differently, the church has only half-
fulfilled the Great Commission. We've gone out
preaching Jesus, but we haven't been able to "teach
them to obey everything" he commanded (Matthew
28:20). As a matter of fact, we haven't paid much attention ourselves to the way of life Jesus taught and
practiced. It hasn't made a noticeable difference in the
way most people live in so-called Christian nations.

That Rwanda, the most thoroughly evangelized
country in Africa, was the site of an unimaginable
genocide is a sign that we have to rethink the notion
of a "Christian nation." But we cannot think critically
about Rwanda without also focusing our energy on
the so-called Christian nations that continue to send
missionaries into the world. What should Christian
missions look like after the Rwandan genocide? In the
aftermath of colonialism, how should Christians engage the social systems that we are part of?

These questions are made more urgent by the main
point of the last chapter—that the stories of politics

93

and economics form us more deeply than we usually care to admit. The political and economic institutions in which we participate both demand and determine our lives. They shape our identities. They demand our total allegiance. What difference, then, does being a Christian make? How can a Christian relate to the political and economic processes and institutions so that Christianity makes a real difference?

In the West, these questions of Christian social engagement are often framed in terms of church-state relations. The basic idea has been that there are two institutions—one called "church" and another called "state"—which are separate in purpose and function, but nevertheless must relate to one another in public life. The growth of religious pluralism has further convinced modern thinkers that their forbearers in Europe were right to say that there must be a universal foundation for common society—a common ground apart from God or religion. After all, if you want to get along with agnostics and Muslims (just to name two), you can't base public decisions on what Jesus said.

So we have what's called the "separation of church and state." Politics is about how we negotiate our social life through laws, structures, and controls. Religion is about how we negotiate the inner life through systems of belief and mystical experience. In the official rhetoric of this compromise, church and state are separate but equal. Most everyone assumes this is a good thing.

While I think there are good reasons to be critical of this compromise, I'm not proposing an alternative to the separation of church and state. I'm not trying to argue that we could *really* be a Christian nation if we'd just give up this false division and claim our country for Jesus. This is not a book about how to reclaim the Christian nation. Nor is it a book about a new "big idea" for church-state relations.

I'm not very interested in theoretical proposals about how to reorganize society from the top down. Separation of church and state is what we have, and I imagine that it will be the dominant paradigm for years to come. As I said at the beginning, this is a book about bodies. So I'm not trying to just think up a better theory for faithful engagement. I want to talk about postures—about how we position our bodies in relationship to the dominant stories of politics and economics in our time. My conviction is that we do not need a new theory as much as we need to reposition our bodies.

This conviction forces me to look back to Rwanda and examine more closely three main ways in which Christianity has positioned itself vis-à-vis the dominant story of Rwanda. I want to show that these postures, even though they were able to achieve some good throughout the church's history in Rwanda, were insufficient to radically alter the direction of the story that eventually led to the 1994 genocide. Even more important, I want to show how these postures, though still popular today, are not sufficient if Christianity is to offer a genuinely distinct identity in the world.

To say that I find these three postures of Christian social engagement insufficient is not to say that they are un-Christian postures. Quite the opposite: I see them as the predominant Christian postures in our world today. And there is biblical precedent for each of them. In this chapter we will read the story of Rwandan Christianity in light of the biblical story of Christ's passion. I will highlight three biblical characters in that story who are emblematic of the postures of Christian social engagement that I find insufficient. These biblical models were the dominant postures of Christianity in Rwanda. More importantly, they continue to be the dominant postures Christians adopt in relation to politics and economics. We must learn to name and understand them.

The Pious Posture

In the fifteenth chapter of his gospel, Mark introduces Simon of Cyrene with a single verse on Jesus' way to the cross. "A certain man from Cyrene, Simon, the father of Alexander and Rufus, was passing by on his way in from the country, and they forced him to carry the cross" (Mark 15:21). To understand the posture Simon represents, we have to imagine the scene. Jesus has been beaten through the night, dressed in mock royal garb, and paraded through the streets of Jerusalem. It is the eve of Passover, and the streets are packed with crowds who are watching the spectacle, no doubt mocking Jesus and enjoying the irony of his purple robe and crown of thorns.

Jesus is all alone, carrying the burden of his cross on a back that has been shredded by the cords of a whip. No doubt Jesus has fallen to the ground by the time he gets to the city's edge. The soldiers have kicked and prodded him, but they realize he's not going to make it up the hill to Golgotha.

On the road ahead of them, they see a man named Simon, just then coming into town. They call to him as Roman soldiers often did in Jesus' day, demanding that he carry the cross. Simon probably hasn't heard Jesus say, "If anyone forces you to go one mile, go with them two miles" (Matthew 5:41). But Simon is no dummy. These soldiers have swords, and they use them on people who don't obey. So Simon takes up the cross and carries it for Jesus.

Simon is a good man, going about his business when he is pressed into service by the state. Many have noted the great help Simon was to our Lord during his time of deepest need. Simon sacrificially gave of himself, bearing the burden of Jesus' cross. In many ways, Simon is a model of the kind of piety that modern Christianity idealizes. He is compassionate, helping Jesus even before he knows who this condemned man is ("Whatever you did for one of the least of these ... you did for me," Matthew 25:40). He is sincere ("Blessed are the pure in heart," Matthew 5:8). He does not complain ("Consider it pure joy ... whenever you face trials of many kinds," James 1:2). Simon serves at great personal cost, carrying the cross as the soldiers commanded. He is a model of pious obedience.

But Simon never stops to ask why Jesus is being crucified. He does not question the twisted authority that would kill the Author of life. No, Simon's pious posture prevents him from seeing that there are times when we are called to stand up against injustice and not bow to earthly authorities. Simon carried the cross obediently.

There was a lot in the story of Christianity in Rwanda that encouraged this posture. It is often said that Rwandans are very obedient and law-abiding citizens. When the voices of Hutu Power told people to kill their neighbors, many of them obeyed without question. Even those who did not kill assumed that the genocide was an inevitable state of affairs; they stood by watching. And when someone ordered them to kill, they stepped in as if they were following a script that could not be questioned. Sometimes people would even apologize, telling their neighbors they were sorry they had to kill them, that they were only following orders from the government.

Rwandans in general are hesitant to question those in power. As in the case of Simon, obedience is the cardinal virtue of their morality. The church not only encouraged this virtue, but it helped shape it.

The White Fathers who first preached Christianity in Rwanda believed in the trickle-down strategy of evangelism. They worked to convert the king and to educate Tutsis, whom they perceived to be the influencers of society. Evangelical missionaries who came to plant churches in the latter half of the twentieth century reinforced the pious posture among new converts in Rwanda.

By the time 1994 came, many Rwandans had experienced a personal conversion and named Jesus as their Lord. They were, for the most part, faithful church members. But they were unable to question the authority of Hutu Power when it commanded them to kill. Well versed in the posture of obedience, they simply did as they were told.

Like Rwandans, many Christians in the West assume the pious posture when relating to political authority. This posture assumes that the gospel is primarily a spiritual message directed toward the hearts of individual women and men. Christians who assume this posture may appear to be apolitical, but they do not necessarily think their faith is politically irrelevant. The gospel, they believe, does indeed have social implications, but the effects of the gospel are made manifest as individual lives are transformed. Personal salvation is the starting point for all social change. Therefore, evangelism is seen as the primary work of the church in the world.

Those who assume the pious posture value obedience, but they need not be meek. Often they are bold in their faith, using social influence to invite political leaders to experience a personal relationship with Jesus. One operating principle of this posture is that the gospel, once accepted in the hearts of the politically powerful, will trickle down to the rest of society. Resources and energy are directed toward evangelistic efforts aimed at people of influence. If the chief of a tribe converts, he will bring his tribe with him. If the president of a nation becomes a born-again Christian, the gospel will somehow trickle down to the nation's citizens. Many evangelical leaders, such as Billy Graham and Bill Bright, have maintained this posture with integrity. They have been consistent, but they have also consistently failed to question prevailing assumptions about the way things are.

The Political Posture

John's story of Jesus' passion presents us with another posture—that of the official from the temple guard. Beginning in John 18:19–22, we read:

Meanwhile, the high priest questioned Jesus about his disciples and his teaching.

"I have spoken openly to the world," Jesus replied. "I always taught in synagogues or at the temple, where all the Jews come together. I said nothing in secret. Why question me? Ask those who heard me. Surely they know what I said."

When Jesus said this, one of the officials nearby slapped him in the face. "Is this the way you answer the high priest?" he demanded.

Though it took a political decision to sentence Jesus to death, John makes clear that there were religious leaders who worked with the political authorities to ensure his prosecution. At the beginning of this text, the high priest calls Jesus in for questioning. He wants him to justify his message and defend the actions of his followers. But Jesus refuses. He has not been teaching in secret, he insists. Ever since coming to Jerusalem, he has talked openly in the temple court. "Your people were there," Jesus says, in effect. "I don't need to repeat myself. If you want to know what I said, ask them."

One of "them," an official of the temple guard, notes Jesus' tone of disrespect and slaps him across the face. His is the sort of rage a mother might be incited to when an insolent child talks back. Jesus has offended this official's deepest convictions. He has touched a nerve deep down inside this guard. It is an outburst of raw human emotion. But the scene is instructive because the guard models what has become another way of Christian social engagement—the political posture.

Notice how this guard defends the power of the high priest. He believes in a religious faith that is politically engaged, and he is deeply offended when Jesus does not respect the recognized authority. You might say this religious official is even more zealous in his defense of the political establishment than some non-Jewish authorities. After all, the gospels suggest that Pilate, the Roman governor in Jerusalem, was reluctant to crucify Jesus. But this guard, trying to defend the high priest's authority, is eager to put Jesus in his place and lead him to his death. Modeling the political posture, this temple guard demonstrates well its cardinal virtue: loyalty.

Loyalty to the governing authorities characterized many of the church's leaders in Rwanda during the genocide. An archbishop of the church sat on the government's ruling council throughout the genocide. Father Wenceslaus, whose story I told in chapter 2, handed over the refugees in his care when the authorities came for them (while carrying a pistol himself). On August 2, 1994, after most of the killing was over, twenty-nine Catholic priests wrote a letter to the pope in which they denied Hutu responsibility for the genocide.

For many Christians in Rwanda, loyalty to the government not only meant they stood by while the genocide happened; often it meant they actively encouraged it, even taking up weapons themselves to kill fellow Christians who had been labeled "cockroaches."

The political posture is a realist's approach to Christian social engagement. It assumes that the world is not perfect, but it is the way it is. Faith must be politically engaged, using the power that is available to the church to do the most good possible. The political posture takes responsibility for the world as it is and does not worry about compromising itself by getting involved in the systems and processes of this world. It knows that people are not perfect but believes the world would be less evil if God's people ran things well.

In the West, many who hold this posture assume the tenets of democracy uncritically. The role of the church, they say, is to ensure the spread of democratic capitalism for the good of the whole world. The political posture leads people to stand boldly for human rights and development in poor countries. It cries out against torture and human trafficking while also encouraging microfinance and antiretroviral drugs in Africa. It suggests that the church's role is to help shape national political dialogue, while remaining a neutral party that can mediate between the various political positions to achieve the best possible synthesis. (In the US, for example, the political posture calls Republicans and Democrats to work together to end poverty.)

Contemporary representatives of the political posture spend much of their time typing advocacy statements and pastoral letters to their representatives in Congress. Many—though not all—are patriotic, even when they are critical. And like the temple guard, they are offended by anyone who disrespects the recognized authority or questions loyalty to the nation state or democratic ideals.

The political posture is often described as "progressive" in conversations about Christian political engagement today, but I must note that activists who assume this posture towed the party line of their nation states while the world watched nearly a million people die in Rwanda.

Stressing the virtues of loyalty and responsibility, the political posture does not push the church to imagine possibilities beyond those the ruling authorities name. Yes, it inspires Christians to do good work. But it accepts the terms of debate as given and chooses sides. At its worst, it stirs up religious conviction to motivate citizens of nation states to promote a political ideology at any cost.

One final note about the political posture: it is almost always rewarded with the spoils of power. Just as the high priest received favors from the Roman authorities and the temple guard benefited, no doubt, from a decent salary, politically postured Christians in the world today receive grants from private foundations and government agencies. These financial resources afford advocacy groups opportunities that they would not have otherwise. The cost, however, may be the promise of loyalty. Those who accept Rome's money usually end up playing by Rome's rules. With some practice, they learn to react violently against anyone who questions the established authority.

The Pastoral Posture

The final posture we'll look at in this chapter is modeled by Joseph of Arimathea. John 19:38–42 records that after Jesus died, Joseph and Nicodemus came to bury his body:

> Later, Joseph of Arimathea asked Pilate for the body of Jesus. Now Joseph was a disciple of Jesus, but secretly because he feared the Jewish leaders. With Pilate's permission, he came and took the body away. He was accompanied by Nicodemus, the man who earlier had visited Jesus at night. Nicodemus brought a mixture of myrrh and aloes, about seventy-five pounds. Taking Jesus' body, the two of them wrapped it, with the spices, in strips of linen. This was in accordance with Jewish burial customs. At the place where Jesus was crucified, there was a garden, and in the garden a new tomb, in which no one had ever been laid. Because it was the Jewish day of Preparation and since the tomb was nearby, they laid Jesus there.

The crucifixion is complete. Jesus has been stripped, beaten, whipped, and hung on a rugged cross. Seeing that he is already dead, a soldier had pierced his side with a spear to let the bodily fluids spill out. Now, under the cover of night, Joseph of Arimathea comes to ask the Roman authority for Jesus' body. It has been abused to the point that there is no life left in it, but it is still the body of a man whom Joseph loved.

Joseph wants to care for Jesus' body — to treat it tenderly, embalm it according to custom, wrap it in fine linen, and give it a proper burial. With his friend Nicodemus, Joseph lays the body of Jesus in a tomb to rest. You can almost feel the gentleness — the reverence — with which these two men perform the last rites. But we do not hear them ask one another, "Who did this to our Lord?" We do not hear the question, "Why?" They are a perfect example of what I call the pastoral posture.

As a pastor, I know this posture well. As with the other two postures, those of us who assume the pastoral posture are well-intentioned and do good work. We are often called to play the role of the Good Samaritan in society. After nation states or paramilitaries or revolutionary forces have done their damage, the church comes in to do its works of mercy. We build schools. We run hospitals. We set up soup kitchens and refugee camps. We bury the dead. We offer last rites to the victims of violence and oppression. Attending to the bodies of people who've been beaten and broken, we practice the pastoral posture's cardinal virtue: compassion.

True to its pastoral role, the church was a major social player in Rwanda. Priests educated the nation's elite in church schools. Of course, these were also the schools where Rwandans learned the racial ideology of the Hamitic story. Though they educated people who might not have had the same opportunities otherwise, it is fair to say in retrospect that these schools became incubators of hatred. In light of this history, it is not quite so ironic that these places of compassionate care became the sites of killing during the genocide.

Often governments in so-called Christian nations will outsource compassion work to the churches, giving us money to perform the social services that are needed in society. So the pastorally postured church understands itself to be in a certain partnership with the state. They do their work; we do ours.

But as Martin Luther King Jr. noted in his now famous sermon, we who play the role of Good Samaritan do not often stop to ask how we might improve conditions on the road to Jericho so that the next person who comes along won't get jumped by a band of robbers. The pastoral posture does not allow our compassion to lean that far into the conditions that create people's need.

The tragedy, of course, is that we stand aside while

the demonic cycle of death-dealing steals, kills, and destroys the bodies and souls of people. In the spring of 1994, Rwandan priests served communion to members of their parishes who took a break from killing to attend worship services. Their hypocrisy is evident to all of us. What we do not see as clearly, however, is how a military chaplain blesses unjust wars while baptizing traumatized soldiers or how a ministry to the homeless accepts the economic assumptions of a system that continues to make people poor. Our pastoral posture trains us to meet the immediate needs of people without asking too many questions.

Is There Another Way?

Let me be clear about what I'm *not* saying. I'm not saying that people who assume the pious, political, and pastoral postures are un-Christian. Each of these postures is rooted in some biblical truth. Whatever doubts I may have about these postures after Rwanda, I still have to deal with the biblical mandates upon which they are based.

Also, I am not saying that the work of inviting people into relationship with Jesus, advocating for political reform, and taking care of real human needs is unnecessary. All of these things are important. What I am saying is that, taken together, they are not enough. They were not enough to keep Christians from killing their fellow Christians in Rwanda. And they are not enough to keep Christians in the West from perpetuating death-dealing political and economic systems.

If Western Christians examine themselves in the mirror that is Rwanda, they will have to acknowledge that the fundamental question of the twenty-first century is not whether people have heard the gospel or how Christians are to gain influence in society. The most pressing question for the church in the twenty-first century is what difference does Christianity make?

What difference does Jesus make when our presidents name other people as the "enemy"? What difference does the gospel make when nations go to war? What difference does church membership make when government authorities tell us what is good and what is bad? What difference does a personal relationship with Jesus make when advertisers tell us what we should desire? What difference does the Bible make when the market tells us what is a good investment of our time and resources?

These are the questions we have to ask after Rwanda. These are the questions that push us to find a new posture in society.

The three postures above do not question—let alone interrupt—the dominant story of politics that allows the church to grow and "Christian influence" to spread. While the church seemed to be flourishing in

Rwanda, bodies were shaped by a dominant ideology of hatred that went unchecked.

Rwanda has pushed global Christianity to a breaking point. It is not enough to re-evangelize Rwanda with the same postures of social engagement that were offered in the past. Rwanda has exposed the hidden lies of Christendom. But it has also revealed our shared need for a new way to live as Christians in the world. It is not enough to be pious, to be safe and obedient, or to be compassionate and kind. The church in Rwanda did not lack any of these. Much more is at stake if we are to reclaim the lordship of Christ and live as ambassadors of God's new creation in the world.

Is there another way? This is the question I want to consider for the remainder of this book. But I don't want to answer too quickly. For I fear that after pointing out the contradictions of those who have tried to make a difference in the world, I will be construed as an idealist, inviting people to dream an impossible dream outside the confines of reality. This is, of course, why the so-called realists always win the argument in the end. Everyone knows that, however good the best of all possible worlds may sound, we live and move and have our being in the one real world we've got.

But I am not an idealist. I am a kingdom realist. The hope I want to point to is not out of this world, because "the Word became flesh and made his dwelling among us" (John 1:14). Jesus announced and established a new political order in this world and called it "the kingdom of God." It is not an ideal that we might achieve one fine day in the sweet by and by. God's kingdom is a reality into which Jesus invites us *now*. When we trust Jesus and do the things he commanded, the kingdom of God is among us. By the power of the Holy Spirit, we are able to stand and assume a new posture.

Despite the horrors of triumphalistic missionary endeavors and so-called Christian nations, I must say something that may sound paradoxical. Modern Christianity has been plagued by a false humility.

True, Christianity has been overconfident in its crusades for land, power, and disembodied souls. We have abused power in the name of Jesus and gone to battle with crosses on our shields. Yet behind all of the posturing this process entailed, we have lacked boldness in the pursuit of our greatest hope: the kingdom Jesus proclaimed.

We have been too easily satisfied as long as we have been allowed to make some small difference in the world, as long as we have been able to achieve some limited good. We have been happy to settle for this in exchange for allowing the basic patterns of the world to go on unchallenged. Expressing this sentiment, G. K. Chesterton once said, "Christianity has not been tried and found wanting; it hasn't been tried."

How do we even begin?

I suggest that we turn again to Scripture, which

offers another posture of Christian social engagement in the world. I also suggest that we turn again to Rwanda, where we can see examples of this form of radical engagement.

CHAPTER 6

Interruptions

Nyamirambo Mosque, Kigali

TOWARD THE END OF MATTHEW'S GOSPEL, A WOMAN WHO John calls Mary interrupts a dinner party in Bethany to anoint Jesus with some very expensive perfume. It's an odd story made even stranger by Jesus' comment after the fact: "Truly I tell you, wherever this gospel is preached throughout the world, what she has done will also be told, in memory of her" (Matthew 26:13).

Jesus says that the good news of God's kingdom cannot be preached without telling the story of Mary who was crazy enough to interrupt. That is a striking statement when you stop to think about it. Judging from the practice of the church, Matthew 26:13 may be one of the most overlooked verses in all of Scripture. I have heard many evangelists preach the gospel a thousand different ways, inviting people to trust Jesus and become part of God's family. But to be quite honest, I can't remember a single evangelist summarizing the gospel message in a way that included Mary's story.

But Jesus says that wherever *his* gospel is preached, Mary's story must be told. It's almost enough to make you wonder whether we've really heard the gospel Jesus came to proclaim.

Why is Mary's interruption so important to our understanding of the good news? What does she have to teach us? Her act is recorded in a single sentence: "While Jesus was in Bethany ... a woman came to him with an alabaster jar of very expensive perfume, which she poured on his head as he was reclining at the table" (Matthew 26:6–7). So far as we know, Mary doesn't say anything. She doesn't draw attention to herself. In Matthew, she isn't even named. But Jesus says her act is essential to the gospel story. So what's going on here?

Maybe we can find a clue in the response of Jesus' disciples. When they saw what Mary was doing, Matthew says they were indignant. "'Why this waste?' they asked. 'This perfume could have been sold at a high price and the money given to the poor'" (Matthew 26:8–9).

Not only has Mary interrupted social norms by barging into a dinner party and dousing a man with oil; the disciples suggest she has also disrupted their economic assumptions. In addition to being out of place, Mary is out of her mind, wasting resources that could have been better allocated elsewhere.

Furthermore, any Jew who knew their Torah would have realized that Mary's act was politically loaded. Like Samuel anointing David the shepherd boy just in

from his father's fields, Mary assumes a prophetic posture and anoints Jesus to be king of her people. She has
not been given the authority to do this. Jesus' name
isn't on the ballot (and besides, even if it were, she
doesn't have a vote). But Mary dares to question the
social, economic, and political assumptions of her day
with a single act. She is crazy enough to *interrupt*.

I believe Mary represents the "rebel consciousness"
that is essential to Jesus' gospel. Wherever the gospel
is preached, we must remember that its good news will
make you crazy. The good news of God's kingdom will
force you to question social norms. Jesus will put you
at odds with the economic and political systems of our
world. This gospel will force you to act, interrupting
the world as it is in ways that make even pious people
indignant.

It is, of course, no accident that we often forget
Matthew 26:13. We would be more comfortable with
a story that did not include Mary's prophetic posture.
But Jesus says that wherever his gospel is preached, her
interruption must be remembered.

Notice how concrete Mary's act is. As I mentioned
before, she doesn't have to say a word. She is not advocating a position or arguing for an idea. No, she repo-
sitions her very body as a prophetic sign. She crosses
boundaries, transforming the aroma and atmosphere of
the room with a single act of devotion.

Without attempting to win influence over anyone,

Mary has forced everyone in the room to check their assumptions. Without grasping for political power, she has pledged her allegiance to God's kingdom. Without accepting the system that would put Jesus to death, she has nevertheless prepared his body for burial. What she meant for coronation also serves as final preparation: "When she poured this perfume on my body," Jesus says, "she did it to prepare me for burial" (Matthew 26:12). Like Joseph of Arimathea, Mary does the pastoral work of preparing Jesus' body. But she does it *before* Jesus dies. The rebel consciousness of a prophetic posture teaches us to rethink not only our mind-set and our approach, but also our timing.

Prophetic Interruptions in Rwanda

Sister Felicitee Niyitegeka was a member of the Auxiliaries of the Apostolate, a religious order of the Catholic Church in Rwanda. She was in charge of an orphanage in the remote town of Gisenyi, where she cared for children, most of whom were Tutsi. When news of the genocide spread to Gisenyi, Felicitee hid over thirty Tutsis in her home and helped many more Tutsis flee over the border into the Congo.

Sister Felicitee's brother, who was an army colonel, asked her to stop protecting Tutsis, but she refused. When the *interahamwe* came to Gisenyi, they told Felicitee that she would be spared because of her brother, but the others in her home would be killed. She answered that her household would have to stay together—in life or in death.

In an attempt to make her recant and save her own life, the *interahamwe* shot each person in front of Felicitee. But she did not waver. When all of her companions had been slaughtered before her, Felicitee asked to be killed. The militia leader told her to pray for him before he shot her.

Sister Felicitee embodies the prophetic posture. In the midst of a genocide that seemed natural to so many, she improvised a powerful interruption. Sheltering Tutsis and helping refugees across the border, she negotiated political boundaries while at the same time refusing to accept their assumptions. She knew the moment when the *interahamwe* came that it was time for her to stand with brothers and sisters who had been marked for death. To the very end, she dared to question the line between her and the militia leader by praying that God would have mercy on him.

In Rwanda Sister Felicitee has been given the title "hero of the nation." Maybe "hero" is the best language nations have for naming the gifts given them by God. But in the church, we call Sister Felicitee a saint and a martyr.

Whereas heroes can be held up only as exceptional human beings, saints are remembered in the church because they are witnesses of God's faithfulness throughout every generation. God has not abandoned the church. Even in the midst of genocide, God gives gifts to help us remember what the church is called to be. Like the woman at Bethany, Sister Felicitee offers a model for us to learn from.

But Sister Felicitee was not alone in Rwanda. The Saint-Paul Pastoral Center in Kigali, where Father Sibomana fought to have refugees welcomed, was able to shelter nearly two thousand Tutsis and moderate Hutus when the genocide began. A week after the killings started, however, police came with arrest warrants for opponents of Hutu Power. Sibomana knew that he was on the assassins' list because of his outspoken protest against human rights abuses over the years.

Early on the morning of April 12, Father Sibomana got in a car with two Tutsi nuns and a fellow priest and drove out of town. Miraculously, they were able to pass through two roadblocks, racing through the first and finding a soldier who was a friend of Sibomana's at the second. Sibomana drove to the small village where he had grown up and went into hiding, moving from house to house without staying in one place very long.

Sibomana spoke to members of the local parish, begging them to resist Hutu Power and love their neighbors as themselves. But the *interahamwe* distributed money and machetes in the little village, and soon the killing started. At one point, Sibomana nearly died from drinking poisoned communion wine.

Father Sibomana's life became a struggle for survival. During a worship service on June 12, his parish was attacked by the *interahamwe*. The congregation fought back against their attackers, and only five Tutsis were taken. The militia men threw them alive into a well in the churchyard. After they had left, someone from the church heard a voice crying out of the well. Father Sibomana and another priest lowered a rope and pulled out two survivors under the cover of night and nursed them back to health.

Despite his courage and willingness to act, Father Sibomana felt the pain of the church's brokenness. "I cannot take any credit for having saved a few people, because I had the power to do so.... During this tragedy, each of us was alone with our conscience."[1] Even those members of the body of Christ in Rwanda who survived were dismembered figuratively, left on their own to discern how to respond to a storm of madness. Acts of courage and resistance were indeed interruptions of the norm.

"There shouldn't have been 'acts of resistance,'" Sibomana reflected years after the genocide. "Resistance should have been the rule and crime the exception. That is not what happened."[2]

Father Wenceslas, meanwhile, knew that no one at Saint-Famille Church was safe. He relied on a pistol for his own survival, but he could not guarantee his mother's safety. The safest place he knew of was the

Hôtel des Mille Collines, just a few hundred yards up the hill from Saint-Famille.

There Paul Rusesabagina, the hotel manager, welcomed those in danger as guests, assigning them to rooms and treating them like his usual international clientele. As I mentioned at the beginning of the first chapter, Paul's story has been beautifully told in the movie *Hotel Rwanda*. As that film depicts so well, Paul was a master of negotiation. He knew the power that every person carries with them in their tongue, and he used his to save the lives of hundreds. When asked how he was able to do this, Paul consistently answers that he doesn't understand why everyone could not have done what he did.

Paul and the Mille Collines provide a striking contrast to Father Wenceslas and the Saint-Famille Church. Both places, of course, provided shelter and saved many lives. But while Father Wenceslas resigned himself to the "time of a pistol" and sacrificed whomever he had to along the way, Paul Rusesabagina carved out a space that became an interruption to the genocide.

The Hôtel des Mille Collines was not simply a refuge. It became a place where people lived with a different set of assumptions, defying the madness of Hutu Power. We should pay careful attention to the fact that, in the midst of genocide, an international hotel offered more good news than the nearest church. Indeed, the Hôtel des Mille Collines offers an example of what the church is called to be—a hopeful interruption to the death-bound reality of a broken world.

This hotel was not the only interruption. Historian Gerard Prunier has noted that the Muslim community of Nyamirambo on the outskirts of Kigali was a consistent interruption to the madness of the genocide. Not only did people there refuse to divide themselves between Hutu and Tutsi, but as a community they protected their Tutsi members when the *interahamwe* came threatening violence.

What is striking about the story of Nyamirambo is not so much that it was a Muslim community as that it was called "Nyamirambo." In the Kinyarwanda language, *Nyamirambo* means "a place of dead bodies." I do not know for sure when or why the place was given this name, but if you visit this dirty slum on the outskirts of Kigali, near the central prison, it is not hard to imagine why it would be called a mortuary.

Yet it was there in a place of death that a minority Muslim community found its home along the margins of Rwandan society. And it was there that they were able to exist as an interruption to the extreme violence of Easter week 1994. Father Sibomana said that each member of the church was left alone with their own conscience. But the Muslims at Nyamirambo stuck together. They, and not the Christian churches, embodied the hope of Christ's resurrection.

Ministry from the Margins

By acting *before* the authorities kill Jesus, the woman at Bethany teaches us a different sense of timing. But she also models the prophetic posture by coming to Jesus at Bethany—that is, *outside* Jerusalem. This woman knows that location matters. She is able to question assumptions and step out of bounds because of where she is. The world looks different from where she is standing. She does not assume a "Capitol Hill imagination." Her witness is political, but it does not accept the common wisdom that everything political has to happen in Jerusalem and on Jerusalem's terms. No, she can pledge her allegiance to Jesus in Bethany. And she can do it with her whole being.

We must take seriously the perceived irrelevance of this woman's location. It is an affront to almost everything we assume in churches about where we should position ourselves in order to responsibly wield influence in society. Too often, modern Christianity has been obsessed with relevance.

I already mentioned the problem of false humility in our churches, which results in Christians not daring to take the gospel seriously. At the root of this false humility, however, may be an insecurity that pushes us to strive for relevance in a world that doesn't think it needs God.

Each of the three postures we looked at in the

previous chapter tries at some point to justify itself in terms of relevance. The pious posture insists that people have real spiritual needs that need to be met, even if they don't realize it. So Christians are taught to position themselves to meet "spiritual" needs in crisis situations (through chaplaincy, for example) or to create contexts where people come to recognize these needs in themselves for the first time (through one-on-one witnessing or evangelistic crusades, for example). It's worth noting that this posture almost always assumes that the church needs to be "where things are happening" so it can meet spiritual needs as they arise. Ministry easily becomes a middle-class profession for clergy or a nights-and-weekends hobby for laypeople.

The political posture is equally transparent in its assertion that Christians ought to locate themselves in places of influence, not so much to meet spiritual needs as to shape social policy. Churches open advocacy offices in Washington, DC, or at the UN. We send our young people to get a top-flight education at the best universities and take jobs in the upper echelons of government, financial institutions, and nongovernmental organizations. Whatever political party we align ourselves with, we want them to know that we are a significant part of their constituency and that they must listen to us. Interestingly, however, we rarely have anything new to say to them. We just want to be sure that our voice is heard (or, even better, quoted in tomorrow morning's paper).

At first glance, it may seem that Christians who assume the pastoral posture are, like the woman at Bethany, conceiving ministry from the margins. We are, after all, in the war zones, the ghettos, the prisons, and the refugee camps of the world. Our location suggests we might see the world differently. But in our pastoral posture, we almost always see ourselves as ministers *to* the margins. We maintain a Capitol Hill imagination by seeing ourselves as bridge people, delivering resources from the generous and powerful to those less fortunate. Unfortunately, this means that we do not often turn around in our places of ministry to reimagine the world *from* the margins. In our attempts to remain relevant, we keep a constant eye on our Blackberry to get the latest news from Washington.

The prophetic posture modeled by the woman at Bethany invites us to rethink relevance—which is to say that it almost always challenges us to relocate ourselves in order to see the world anew. The transformation of Archbishop Oscar Romero in El Salvador is a good example of how a little perspective can radically change one's posture. Romero was elected archbishop of El Salvador in the politically tumultuous 1970s. A well-educated member of El Salvador's upper class, Romero was a safe pick for those in charge—or so they thought. No one suspected he would rock the boat.

But when his friend and fellow priest Rutillio Grande was killed by government soldiers in the village of Aguilares, Romero journeyed from the capital city to recover the body of his friend.

What Romero saw and heard in that place changed him. He knew that his ministry was now to speak out against the injustices of a government that was run by people he knew and had dinner with. Ultimately, this ministry cost Romero his life.

Romero is an example of how we can be converted to the prophetic posture. Such a conversion changes our mind-set in society, prepares us to receive the kingdom now, and calls us to reimagine ministry from the margins. We need examples like that of Romero if we are going to become crazy enough to interrupt the madness that manifested itself in the Rwandan genocide.

I want to conclude this chapter with the story of another woman who performed the prophetic posture faithfully in the midst of Rwanda's story. If Rwanda is to truly be a mirror to the church in the West, we would do well to reimagine ourselves in light of the following story.

Nyamata is a marginal place. When I visited in 1998, I remember noting how it was surrounded by swamps and, as they say in the southern United States, "a million miles from nowhere." The road to Nyamata was terrible, even by Africa standards.

When we were there, a survivor told me the story of how the UN had sent two armored Land Rovers over those roads in the midst of the genocide. When they arrived, thousands of people were taking shelter in the local church, and two Belgian priests and one nun were scrambling to tend to their needs. Whether they knew it or not, these Westerners were keeping the *interahamwe* at bay by their simple presence.

But the Land Rovers had been sent to evacuate all expatriates, so the nun and two priests got into the vehicles and rode back to Kigali to board a plane bound for safety. After they left, the militia descended on the church compound and killed almost everyone. Eight thousand people were buried in a mass grave behind the church.

I remember praying as I stood outside the church at Nyamata, "God, is there any sign of hope in this place?" By the side of the church, I found the marker for a single grave. I was surprised to see an Italian woman's name: Toni Locatelli. I asked our guide about the grave, and he told me Toni's story.

Following the 1990 invasion of Rwanda by the Tutsi-led RPF army, local militias and the police in Nyamata began a systematic process of killing Tutsis. Toni Locatelli, an Italian social worker who had lived there for more than twenty years, alerted the international media about the sporadic but systematic killings that were going on around Nyamata. As a result, the international media descended on Nyamata and reported the killings. The police commander was so infuriated by the media's presence that he shot Toni Locatelli. She was buried by the side of the church.

The fact that Toni lies buried in Nyamata alongside other (Rwandan) victims of genocide is, I believe, a sign of hope. Her presence and sacrifice redefine the concept of "my people." Like the witness of a martyr, her story announces the power of Christ's resurrection to create a new communion beyond black and white.

In a world marked by neat and settled identities that divide Christians, Toni's story of interruption—like those of the Hôtel des Mille Collines and the Muslim community at Nyamirambo—is a sign of hope. Without stories like these, we cannot begin to imagine church as a resurrected and strange communion of witnesses drawn from all tribes, nations, and languages.

But such sanctified imagination is precisely what the church is called to in this world. To enter into the pain of the Rwandan genocide and feel it as our own is to begin to see how our minds have become captive to the powers of this world.

At the same time, the interruptions witnessed in these stories teach us something about the nature of the church's vocation in the world. After all, these stories are not simply examples of heroic decisions and actions. They reveal the formation of a certain type of identity at work. They point to individuals and communities that are grounded in an identity that goes beyond Hutu or Tutsi, white or black, Western or African. You might even say these examples reveal a certain kind of *confused* identity.

What would it mean to bear such a confused identity? This may be the most important question Rwanda teaches us to ask. So I want to devote the next chapter to a consideration of what makes the prophetic posture possible.

Making a Prophetic
Posture Possible

Carl Wilkens, US missionary to Rwanda

I AM A GOSPEL PRAGMATIST.

I know that critical engagement with the world is important, and careful consideration of the biblical story is essential. I realize that inspiring sermons and the lives of the saints can be a great help to the church. But at the end of the day, I want to know how we are going to live out the good news that we have seen and heard.

As part of my work with Duke Divinity School's Center for Reconciliation, I facilitated a convocation in 2007 for church leaders from the Great Lakes region of Africa. It was a time of rest and renewal for pastors and activists whose tireless work can easily become all-consuming. We tried to help these church leaders step back and take the long view—to put the everyday work of their parishes and communities in the context of God's greater plan to redeem the world. We asked them to pay attention to the deeper questions that they didn't have time to think about in the midst of their everyday responsibilities. We asked them to consider God's bigger vision for the church in that region.

I will never forget the testimony of Bishop Emmanuel Kolini at the end of our week together. He told the story of how he had grown up as an exile in the Congo, a Rwandan refugee of mixed parentage. When he was appointed bishop of the Anglican church in Rwanda after the genocide in 1994, he talked to the priests in his diocese and heard the stories of those who had lived through the horror. He told us how as he listened he began to feel the weight of their history of violence.

"I realized that almost everyone in our churches had killed," Bishop Kolini said. "Even the priests had killed." After our week of reading Scripture and reflecting together on God's vision for the church, Bishop Kolini said, "This is my question: how do we become a church of people who can say no to killing?"

Whether we are in Rwanda or the United States, the reality we have to face is that we do not have many churches that are able to say no. When genocide is happening, we do not know how to resist. When conspicuous consumption is the norm, we are not very good at living an alternative.

But the witness of the biblical story is that God's people are always invited to say no to the idols of their age and rise up by the power of the Spirit as a holy interruption. This chapter is about the who, what, where, why, and how of prophetic witness. Paying attention to Rwanda as a sign of the times, we can feel the urgency of our global situation. We need an alternative.

The examples of interruption we considered at the end of the last chapter—Sister Felicitee, the Muslim community at Nyamirambo, Toni Locatelli—all suggest that another way *is* possible. These examples are signs that point us to God's hope for the world. We don't need just *any* change. We need prophetic interruptions that point to God's new creation.

But the gospel pragmatist in me wants to get down to brass tacks. Who's going to do it? What does it look like? When will it happen? Where and how? If we're going to make a prophetic posture possible in our own lives, we need to think through these very practical questions.

Who We Are:
Reclaiming Our Resident Alien Status

I noted in chapter 2 that the United States embassy evacuated all American civilians from Rwanda at the beginning of the genocide in 1994. They were told that it was no longer safe for them to be there. Diplomats, businesspeople, tourists, and missionaries alike boarded planes at the airport in Kigali and left Rwanda behind. Except for Carl Wilkens.

Carl Wilkens had worked in development and relief

work in Rwanda for four years and in Africa for ten years. He was the only American citizen who did not leave Rwanda during the genocide. He stayed in Kigali, the capital city where he had been working, and did what he could to bring food, medicine, and water to several groups of orphans around the city. One particular day during the slaughter, Wilkens found himself and more than two hundred orphans surrounded by the *interahamwe* militia, fifty men armed with machetes and assault rifles clearly intent on killing them all. Calling for help and having seven soldiers respond, he left the orphanage in their care and went looking for more help. In a chance meeting at a local government office, Wilkens was able to plead the case of the orphans to the "bogus" prime minister (who was later convicted of genocide crimes). Though Wilkens had no power to defend against the *interahamwe*, the orphanage was mysteriously spared. The *interahamwe* never came in.[1]

What most impresses me about Wilkens is that somehow he understood that he was a resident alien in Rwanda. He was not Rwandan, of course. He had not been marked as Hutu or Tutsi. As an outsider, he was able to see through these identities and insist they were not the most important markers of who somebody was. Genocide was not normal. It could neither be accepted nor blamed on tribalism or ancient conflicts.

Wilkens's alien status enabled him to recognize the

strangeness of genocide. Yet unlike other Americans, he had somehow located himself within Rwanda as a resident. These were his people. He could not abandon them in the midst of chaos. Their troubles were his, so he chose to stay. He was a resident alien, embodying the biblical injunction to be both strange and local at the same time.

In 2 Corinthians 5:20 the apostle Paul writes, "We are ... Christ's ambassadors, as though God were making his appeal through us." To the question, "Who are we?" Paul answers: We are Christ's ambassadors. As ambassadors, we must constantly negotiate the tension of our unique identity. This world is not our home. We are not ultimately defined by its stories or bound by the norms that it assumes. Yet this world is the ground we live on. We have been called to serve here so that God might make his appeal through us.

Ambassadors who represent nations testify to the difficulty of balancing this dual identity. They are constantly pulled between the people they know and love and the government they represent. (Indeed, I am told that the US government recognizes this tension and moves State Department employees every three years in order to prevent the development of bonds that might compromise their loyalty to the United States.) The apostle Paul says this is the tension we are to embrace within the kingdoms of this world.

Whether we live in Rwanda or Belgium or North

Carolina, this world is not our home. We are on a journey, bound for the kingdom where God's justice and peace are the governing order and reigning assumptions. Yet we are called to pray, "Your kingdom come, your will be done *on earth* ..."—right here in the places where we live.

Wherever I am, I must know the people of my parish because my salvation in Christ is bound up with theirs. Eternal life is not something that I enjoy by myself when life in this world is over. I have been saved for life forever *with* other people. That life is possible because of Jesus. But the apostle Paul is clear: the eternal life of Christ's body is a life we share with brothers and sisters who, like us, have been called out of the kingdoms of this world into a new way of life (1 Corinthians 12:12 and following). Either we are saved together or we die as dismembered individuals.

If the church in the twenty-first century is to reposition itself into a prophetic posture, we will have to learn what it means to reclaim our resident alien status. It is not enough for us to live in this world as individuals with spiritual tourist visas, enjoying the scenery while we wait to be raptured home at any moment. We have to live with our feet on the ground, devoted to our calling to serve God in this place.

But we must also resist the temptation to transfer our citizenship from God's kingdom to this world. If we love our neighbors and know their suffering intimately, we will inevitably want to make a difference in their lives (and in ours). The prince of this world will tell us (as he told Jesus in the desert) that we can rule the nations—if only we will transfer our allegiance to him. But we must say with Jesus, "Away from me, Satan! For it is written: 'Worship the Lord your God, and serve him only'" (Matthew 4:10).

Jesus' quotation of Deuteronomy 6:13 is an exhortation to remember who we are as a people engaged in true worship. We cannot underestimate the power of pledging our allegiance to God in prayer and praise, song and sacrament, reading of Scripture and proclamation of the Word. This is how we get the story of God's people down deep in our bones.

I do not think it is any accident that the civil rights movement in the United States grew out of black churches where people were used to worshiping Jesus for two, three, even four hours at a time. Christians who cannot imagine worshiping God that long may want to reconsider their cost/benefit analysis of discipleship. Jesus said that whoever followed him would suffer as he did. The promised reward, so far as I can tell in Scripture, is only that we get to worship God forever. If we can't imagine that as good news on earth right now, I don't suppose the idea of eternal life is good news.

But if we know that worship of the true and living God is what we are made for, we will also remember who we are: a community of resident aliens in a world that is both broken and redeemed. Because we know a new creation in Christ, we will live as ambassadors, welcoming strangers as though we belong here while also praying for the heavenly city, our true home, to descend to where we are.

Where We Are:
Cultivating Wild Spaces in Our World

In real estate they say that the three most important factors are "location, location, location." Much of the church needs a healthy dose of this kind of realism. Often we forget, especially in the West, that we always worship God *somewhere*. Worship is not a merely spiritual reality, somehow separate from the everyday practices of economics, politics, and social life. The life of God's people always happens in some place.

When we see ourselves as resident aliens, we may be tempted to think we could better remember the story of God's people if we could just get away from the television, the Internet, secular radio stations, and public education. We think we could be holy if we just had our own space—some virgin soil on which to plant a truly Christian society.

But the fact of the matter is that there is no virgin soil. We always find ourselves living within social and political systems and stories not of our own making.

And even if there were virgin soil somewhere, none us have virgin minds. Jesus calls us from the midst of this world's system to follow him and learn what true worship means.

Rather than think about relocating to some new place where we can start fresh and get it right, I think the church is called to cultivate "wild spaces" in the midst of this world. This is a phrase I learned from fellow theologian Sally McFague. To explain what she means by it, McFague asks us to imagine the norms and assumptions of conventional Western culture as a circle.

Let's say that our circle defines the boundaries of what is "normal" for white European rationalists who have reaped the benefits of colonialism and a university education. On top of that circle, McFague invites us to imagine a second one, representing the boundaries of our own experience. There are, of course, places where these two circles overlap. My circle, for example, would overlap considerably with the conventional norm, not only because I have learned to survive in the world as it is, but also because I have studied at European universities and worked at American universities.

Nevertheless, because I am a Ugandan, the son of Rwandan exiles, born with black skin and shaped by the stories of my village, there is a large crescent of my circle that does not overlap with the Western circle. McFague says that this is my wild space. This is the space that allows me to question social norms and imagine alternatives. Of course, this wild space sometimes makes my life difficult. But it also opens new opportunities.

Resident aliens who engage in true worship will begin to carve out wild spaces in this world. These will not be perfect communities—far from it. They will, instead, be communities shaped by the story we read in Matthew 14.

Matthew tells us that Jesus retreats to a deserted place, but he is followed by a crowd of people. Knowing they need to hear the good news of the kingdom, Jesus stays and teaches them all day. Now it is late and the disciples come to tell Jesus that he should dismiss the crowd so they can go to town and get something to eat. The lesson is done, the disciples seem to say. These people need to attend to their material needs now.

But Jesus seems to think the lesson has something to do with what people eat. So he says to the disciples, "They do not need to go away. You give them something to eat" (Matthew 14:16).

In the midst of apparent scarcity, Jesus says, in effect, "Don't go anywhere. Wait here. Something new can happen in this place." He takes into his hands the very real stuff of bread and fish and wicker baskets, offering them to God and trusting in a reality deeper than an economics of scarcity. He breaks the bread, and somehow there is more than enough for everyone. "They all ate and were satisfied," Scripture says, "and the disciples picked up twelve basketfuls of broken pieces that were left over" (v. 20).

In the end, there is an abundance in the wild space that is created by Jesus. But it is an abundance of broken pieces. The new reality made possible in wild spaces is not about creating the ideal conditions for a new society. Jesus doesn't turn five thousand stones into whole loaves so that each man can have one for his family. No, the multiplication is in the fragments. God offers us new possibilities as we trust Jesus and begin to work with the fragments where we are.

In November of 1994, after surviving the genocide, Father Andre Sibomana was appointed the administrator of the Kabgayi diocese, the biggest in Rwanda. After the hundred days of genocide, the diocese was in shambles. Some seventy thousand people were on the brink of starvation. Around twenty thousand orphans were left without homes. Hundreds of genocide survivors were in need of medical treatment for machete wounds. All of these problems were piled on top of the reality that hundreds of thousands of people had been brutally murdered. Eighteen of the eighty-seven priests in the diocese had been killed. "We had to rebuild everything," Father Sibomana recalls, "including minds and bodies, public buildings, houses, families ..."[2]

The only people who were left to rebuild were the Tutsi survivors and the Hutus who had killed. Sibomana didn't know how it would be possible, but he knew his job as a priest was to call these people to work together. So he started a program to rebuild homes destroyed by the *interahamwe* raids. Sibomana hired Hutu and Tutsi men to work together on these homes for survivors of the genocide.

At first the workers would not speak to each other. In time, though, as they worked side by side in the debris of genocide, they began to make connections and speak once again. In August 1995, Sibomana organized a celebration to dedicate the first two hundred homes that had been completed. Resting from their work, Hutu and Tutsi workmen drank banana beer from the same jug.[3]

Those workmen drinking from the same jug are a picture of the wild space that the church is called to remember every time we celebrate the Lord's Supper. This is not a meal for perfect people. Every time we eat it, we remember that Jesus inaugurated this meal "on the night he was betrayed" (1 Corinthians 11:23). In the midst of that brokenness, though, Jesus gave himself to the friends who would betray and abandon him. Likewise, when we gather to receive the bread and the wine each week, the church remembers where we are.

We live and move and have our being in the midst of this world's brokenness. We do not flee the world, but rather carve out wild spaces within it. We are a people who can imagine new possibilities because we worship One who took on flesh and joined us where we were.

How We Plan:
The Tactics of Kingdom Leadership

If the church really is going to be a different kind of people, cultivating creative wild spaces, we also have to unlearn the world's way of doing things. Our problem is not just that we chase after the wrong things. Even when we have the right end in mind, we often try to get there by means we have learned from this world's systems.

Many who heard Jesus preach were excited about his vision for a new social order. They were drawn to Jesus' concept of what the kingdom should look like. But when Jesus explained how he intended to get to that end — by dying on a cross — not many of his disciples were prepared to follow. Even Peter, who insisted he would follow all the way, faltered in Gethsemane and denied Jesus during his hour of need.

If we are serious about training ourselves for the prophetic posture, we will have to consider how we've bought into the world's ways of operating. One way I like to talk about this is by making a distinction between strategy and tactics — a distinction I learned from a French philosopher, Michel deCerteau.

Strategy, deCerteau says, is how people in power plan the way they want things to work. Strategy is usually developed around a boardroom table, with input from experts who have thoroughly researched all the relevant data. They analyze a situation from a distance, relying on intelligence reports, the best technology, and conventional wisdom about political and economic policy. Strategy is always realistic, even when it is ambitious. It lays out a step-by-step process for moving with predictable results from where we are to where we want to be.

Strategy is the posture of the powerful. It sets goals and commits to measurable outcomes. It is not comfortable with uncertainties, but always accounts for them as a predictable variable.[4]

On the other hand, tactics are the tools of the weak. Having grown up in Uganda, I am well acquainted with political revolutions. Our government always had a strategy for the future of the country as well as one for the war against insurgents. But the revolutionaries were guerrilla fighters. They did not have the luxury of boardrooms where they could work out a new strategy for Uganda. So they were forced to learn a different way of planning. Guerrillas don't have a strategy. They have tactics.

Tactics are the wisdom of the weak about how to survive in a world they do not own. Tactics assume that the system we live under cannot be reformed or reorganized in its entirety. Instead, tactics plot to subvert the reigning system at those places where it is weak. Tactics are worked out on the fly and passed on in the jungle, under the cover of night. Like strategy, they are realistic, but tactics do not pretend to know for certain what will happen in the future. Tactics depend on the art of improvisation. When situations change, tactics change with them.

The distinction between strategy and tactics helps us to see something about how Jesus taught his disciples to negotiate the systems of this world. The gospels are clear about the fact that Jesus meant to introduce a new political order in the world. Whatever else is meant by "the kingdom of God," it is based on the principal Old Testament image for political order and the basic political unit assumed by Jesus' contemporaries. But the fact that Jesus proposed a new political order did not mean that he presented a strategy for its implementation. Instead, I think most of Jesus' teachings about kingdom leadership sound more like tactics.

"Turn to them the other cheek" (Matthew 5:39) assumed that disciples who pledged their allegiance to God would be slapped by a Roman soldier at some point. Jesus didn't think there was any way out of a power system that tries to keep subjects in their place. (Indeed, we've already looked at the passage where Jesus was slapped by an official of the temple guard.) But Jesus did teach that his disciples could subvert the assumptions of the system and expose its inherent weakness by both refusing the insult and refusing to fight back.

Or consider, for example, Jesus' teaching about economics. Clearly, Jesus was indignant about the system of debt-slavery that was crushing most Jewish people in his day. One of the reasons Jesus was so well received by the masses was because he talked so much about forgiveness of debts. But Jesus did not go to Herod and present a strategy for ending poverty in Galilee. Instead, Jesus taught poor people tactics for subverting the dominant economic order and creating new possibilities within it. "Settle matters quickly with your adversary who is taking you to court," Jesus advised (Matthew 5:25).

You'll do better with a direct personal appeal than at the mercy of an unjust judge, Jesus said, passing on a tactic for people who are stuck in poverty. "I tell you," Jesus said to his disciples, "use worldly wealth to gain friends for yourselves" (Luke 16:9). Because the only hope for survival, Jesus suggests, is to create a new community of generosity in the midst of an oppressive economy.

Maybe we can't change the whole system. But maybe that's not the point. By assuming the mind-set of the powerful, we have neglected the tactical wisdom of Jesus that offers a different way of working for God's kingdom in this world.

When I met Paul Rusesabagina, the manager of "Hotel Rwanda" who sheltered hundreds during the genocide, I was struck by his simple insistence that anyone could have done what he did. While acknowledging that he made use of the connections he had, Paul did not think that his resources or access were particularly unique. "Hundreds of people could have done what I did," he said. "But we so easily forget the power of words."

Paul's tactic of negotiation is what saved the guests at the Hôtel des Mille Collines. Of course, he did not know how he was going to save them when he started talking, but he believed in the power of words to make a difference. Paul knew he had no choice but to start talking and figure out a plan as he went along.

If the church in our time is to assume a prophetic posture, we will have to focus less on effective strategy and more on what Paul Rusesabagina saw—that we have no choice but to step into the deep brokenness of our world, start talking, and figure out what faithfulness means as we go. My suspicion is that if we read the gospels along the way, many of Jesus' teachings that have often sounded strange in the past might begin to sound like they were spoken directly to us.

What We Do:
Christian Witness as Defiance and Resistance

In Africa, when you meet someone for the first time, you ask, "Who is your family?" In Europe, they ask, "Where are you from?" But in America, I never cease to be amazed that people almost always ask, "What do you do?" Of course, the church has to answer this question too. Pastors get used to outlining their ministry programs, talking about the missionaries they support, quoting figures, and counting cars in the parking lot. We want to know that our churches are doing something in society—that we are somehow making a difference.

But if we look into the mirror that is Rwanda, we also have to acknowledge that the difference Christianity makes is not always for the better. Indeed, not just Rwanda, but most of the genocides of the twentieth century were carried out by people who called themselves Christians. Many post-colonial writers from Africa have argued that the Bible is not the Good Book sometimes misread, but rather that it is a Bad Book. Christianity has made Africa more violent, they say. Yes, the church made a difference, but it was a change for the worse.

Christians must take seriously the charge that we have done more harm than good in the world. If we are to continue proclaiming that the gospel is good news, we will have to change what we do. Rather than perform spiritual and social duties that prop up the status quo, we must bear witness to the reality of God's new creation by defying the powers of evil and resisting the divisions society imposes on us. The best way I know to describe what this might look like is to tell the story of a school in Nyange, Rwanda, which I first visited in 2004.

On March 18, 1997, three years after the genocide ended, *interahamwe* militia attacked the secondary school at Nyange. The students had finished supper and their evening prayer and were in their classrooms doing homework at the time of the attack. The rebels barged into two classrooms and asked the students to separate — Tutsi to one side, Hutu to the other. But the students refused, saying they were all Rwandans. The militia shot at them indiscriminately and threw grenades into the classroom. In all, thirteen students were killed. The victims were reclaimed by their families and buried at their homes — except Chantal, who was from Changugu, a long distance away. She was buried at the school. Her tombstone bears this simple inscription:

Chantal Mujjawamaholo.

B.24.04.1975

D. 18.03.1997

She was just a month shy of her twenty-second birthday when she was killed.[5]

Our world is marked by tribal, racial, and national identities. So often these labels define us, and we assume these identities are natural. But the story of Chantal and her friends reveals the idolatrous nature of these so-called natural identities. In her native Kinyarwanda,

Chantal's name "Mujjawamaholo" means "maiden of peace." A stranger from far away, she brought a witness of peace to Nyange by refusing to accept the categories of Hutu and Tutsi. Living out of her confused identity, she was indeed a maiden of peace.

We need Chantal's witness of resistance to remind us that God has already inaugurated a new creation. Of course, not all defiance witnesses to the deeper reality of God's goodness in the world. When we forget the gift God has already given us in Jesus Christ, resistance becomes either a form of reckless self-sacrifice or an expression of radical fundamentalism. Defiance can just as easily be an expression of pride as a witness to God's kingdom. But if we do not have witnesses like the students in Nyange to point the way to God's new creation, we have little reason to hope the world will receive the gospel as good news.

What makes this kind of witness possible? When I visited Nyange's secondary school and heard the story of Chantal Mujjawamaholo and her friends, I asked for explanations of why the students were willing to risk their lives before dividing between Hutu and Tutsi. Where did such courage come from?

A teacher at the school suggested different possibilities, including the fact that the students had just finished their evening prayers and might have drawn spiritual strength from that. But he also told me about another teacher who had taught a course in unity and nonviolence. Every morning before class, this teacher would talk to the students about Martin Luther King and Mahatma Gandhi.

That was all he could think of—the evening prayer and a talk here and there on nonviolence. We don't often think of such acts as witnesses to resistance and defiance. But in a world so enamored with grand strategies to end poverty and eradicate terrorism, Nyange reminds us that resistance is about small acts and gestures—a story here, a lesson there. If only the *interahamwe* had internalized the stories those students knew, genocide might have been avoided.

The church does its work in small acts of everyday faithfulness that point to God's deeper vision. We are not ourselves the exemplification of that vision. The tragedy is that when we try to be a "Christian nation," we end up stamping the world's systems with Jesus' logo. The Muslim scholar Mahmoud Mamdani said of the church in Rwanda that it became an "epicenter that radiated violence."[6]

But we are called to stand as signs in the world that another way is possible. Nation-building is not what we do. Instead, we are called to point to a reality beyond us. Mother Teresa often said, "We can do no great things, only small things with great love." Through a thousand small acts of love and service, we show the world signs of something bigger than us that is nevertheless as real as the flesh and blood of Jesus Christ.

When We Do It:
Living the Kingdom Now

With each of the postures identified in chapter 5, we observed that radical questions about how the world is ordered are put off—delayed indefinitely by the powers that be. The timing is never right. The prophetic posture, however, assumes that the time for faithful action is always now. This posture forces our bodies to interrupt the social order because we cannot afford to wait.

In his "Letter from a Birmingham Jail," Martin Luther King Jr. responded to eight fellow clergymen who had called him an extremist and insisted the timing was not right for direct action against the racist government of Birmingham, Alabama. "For years now I have heard the word 'Wait!'" King wrote. "It rings in the ear of every Negro with piercing familiarity. This 'Wait' has almost always meant 'Never.' We must come to see, with one of our distinguished jurists, that 'justice too long delayed is justice denied.'"[7]

King could not wait any longer because he felt the weight of oppression. The gradualists, it must be said, didn't feel that burden. Those who know the pain of injustice can help us to see the urgency of our situation. We cannot wait, they remind us, because the powers that be are crushing the life out of people. Maybe Mary interrupted the dinner party at Bethany because she had suffered too long.

But the experience of suffering is not the only reality that changes our sense of timing in the world. What is even more important than the experience of suffering is the realization that we do not have to wait any longer because *Jesus is here now.*

Jesus inaugurated the new social order that is coming and has now come in the beloved community of those who trust God and live by the Holy Spirit's power. For anyone who will believe, a new reality is possible now. We are invited to live as interruptions not because we have supernatural power to change the world, but because Jesus has already interrupted the world with his birth, life and ministry, death on a cross, and resurrection. The prophetic posture assumes that we must always take Jesus at his word and live the kingdom life he taught us now.

For the past hundred years or so, Christians in America have debated the timing of God's kingdom in terms of pre- and post-millennialism. The whole debate turns on a particular reading of Revelation that assumes the "millennial reign," or thousand-year rule of Christ on earth, is an event that must happen before the final judgment and the end of history. Assuming this reading, Christians have argued whether (a) the church will be raptured away from the earth before this event or (b) the church is participating in the gradual betterment of society until this present era is fulfilled. The pre-millennialists who believe that society is going to get worse and worse until the church is raptured assume a pious posture in the meantime. The post-millennialists, on the other hand, are more often advocates of the kind of gradualism that the political posture assumes.

What this debate seems to miss entirely, however, is that Jesus invited people to participate in God's kingdom *before* Revelation was ever written. The timing of our response to Jesus does not hinge on whether we're living before or after Jesus' thousand-year reign. God's reign is itself a time when people in particular places are called to interrupt the normal flow of events by trusting Jesus and obeying all the things that he commanded.

The prophetic posture always trusts that the time to worship Jesus and acknowledge him as our king is now. However disturbing that conviction may be to those around us, it is the only option for anyone who has heard and believed this gospel.

Why We Do It:
A New Identity in Christ

The mission of the church is rooted in the mission of God. Second Corinthians 5:17–20 makes clear that God's work in Jesus was to reconcile all things to himself. The deepest truth in the universe is that God has already accomplished this. Ephesians says that the dividing wall of hostility between peoples has already been destroyed (2:14). Galatians says there is no longer male nor female, Greek nor Jew, slave nor free (3:28). This isn't something we hope for God to do in the future. The truth is that God has already done it.

This is why we bother to learn the prophetic posture in the world. Because we are invited to be part of God's new creation now, we seek to embody the identity we have been given in Christ. Accordingly, the goal of mission is not primarily aid (humanitarian assistance); it's not even partnership. We engage in mission to establish friendships that lead to the formation of a new people in the world.

The church's primary purpose is not to make America more Christian, but to make American Christians less American and Rwandan Christians less Rwandan. We are no longer Rwandans or Americans, neither Hutu nor Tutsi. If we are in Christ, we have become part of a new creation.

I cannot forget that Hutu boy who fled to the bush with Tutsis. After two or three weeks they pointed out to him that he was Hutu and did not have to die. He left the marshes and was not attacked. But he had spent so much time with Tutsis that he was mixed up. He was confused. He no longer knew how to draw the "proper" line between the two ethnic groups.

That boy is what Christian mission is about.

We have taken this stuff about tribe, ethnicity, and national identity too seriously. In so many places, it has become idolatry. What we need is a new sense of Christian identity that will cause a much-needed confusion of tribal loyalty. Unless this happens, all our singing and proclamations about Christ are empty words. Unless we are defined by a new identity, all our Easter celebration is nothing but a haunted liturgy, with death, genocide, and betrayal lurking in its shadow.

This who, what, when, where, why, and how of a prophetic posture is my attempt to answer the most basic questions about what it takes to make church happen in our time. These are the sort of questions that bodies have to ask if we are to be Christ's body in the midst of any body politic.

But embodied people do not often function systematically. Sometimes it helps to step back and think through our lives in categories. But asking who, what, when, where, how, and why is not enough. In the end we always live the stories that make us and tell a story with our lives. The story that the church has been telling for two thousand years is an outrageous tale about a man who was executed by the state but rose up from the dead. The crux of the story isn't that Jesus figured out the right answer to all the questions facing Israel in his day. What makes all the difference is that Jesus defeated the ultimate enemy and got up from the dead.

To live as the body of Christ in such a time as this is to reimagine what it means to remember and embody that story of resurrection.

Resurrecting the Church

The destroyed church at Nyange

In the summer of 2007, I lead a group of thirty-one people on a pilgrimage to Rwanda. We visited a number of genocide memorials, including the ones in Kigali and Murambi. We met and talked to many survivors—people who had lost entire families during the genocide. In some cases the people we met had only narrowly survived themselves. During our meetings we talked and prayed together. But much of the time we simply stood together in a heavy silence.

I can never forget the day we visited the genocide memorial at Nyange. We met a survivor, Aloysius Rwamasirabo, who told us what had happened. When the killing started in Nyange on April 12, many people took refuge in the church. They closed and locked the doors. Soon the militia surrounded the church and started throwing grenades and shooting through the windows. They tried to burn the church, but because the walls were made of stone, they did not succeed.

According to Rwamasirabo, that's when the priest, Father Seromba, and a businessman had a meeting. Soon workers brought two bulldozers to the church. One of the drivers asked Father Seromba whether he really wanted him to destroy the church. Father Seromba gave him permission to go ahead, saying that the Hutus were many. "We should be able to build another church," he told the man.

The bulldozers demolished the church, killing nearly three thousand people inside. Rwamasirabo survived because he had sneaked out of the church the night before. For two months he was hidden by some Hutu friends. That is how he survived. But his two children perished. One of the children survived the initial collapse of the church, crawled from the ruins, and went to the parish house to ask for water. But one of the priests notified the militia, and they came and killed the boy.

Rwamasirabo's eldest son was at school when the church was demolished. He was later able to reunite with his mother, and the two hid in a bush. But they were later discovered by the militia and killed. His entire family was destroyed, and Rwamasirabo alone was left to tell us the story.

Listening to Rwamasirabo, I felt tears welling up in my eyes. I was disturbed not only by the pain of the demonic madness that led to the loss of so many lives, but also by the church's betrayal. The church betrayed victims like Rwamasirabo and his family who perished at Nyange. But we also betrayed the perpetrators—the militia and *interahamwe*—to whom the church offered no better story than the one they perpetuated.

I asked Rwamasirabo if he still came to church. His answer was, "No. I do not want to believe anymore in religion and in priests. But I do believe in God."

Rwamasirabo keeps the keys of the ruined church, which has now been made into a genocide memorial. After sharing his story, he opened the big metallic gate for us to go into the enclosed open space that was once the church. At the back of the memorial, in the place where the church sacristy once stood, there was a memorial wall with over forty-five skulls and other remains.

As Rwamasirabo explained how the bulldozers had scooped up bodies to bury them, we realized we were standing on top of one of the mass graves, which happened to mark the very place where the altar had been in the church. This was holy ground. I asked Rwamasirabo if it would be okay for us to pray there.

We all knelt on top of the mass grave. Asking everybody to hold hands, I found myself praying for forgiveness from those below the altar. "We killed you," I whispered. "Please forgive us. You did not die because you were Christians. You died in spite of your being Christian, betrayed by the very church you loved and trusted."

As I prayed to the dead and to God for forgiveness, the words of Revelation 6:9–10 came to me, which I read aloud:

> When he [the angel] opened the fifth seal, I saw under the altar the souls of those who had been slain because of the word of God and the testimony they had maintained. They called out in a loud voice, "How long, Sovereign Lord, holy and true, until you judge the inhabitants of the earth and avenge our blood?"

"How long?" asked the souls of those who had been slaughtered. Like Abel's blood, their souls cried out in the words of Scripture. I could almost hear those slain at Nyange say it from beneath the altar: "How long?" I echoed their prayer with my own—"How long?"—and prayed that those below the altar might move us to join them in this cry of lament. "How long, O Sovereign Lord?"

At Nyange it became clear to me that the resurrection of the church begins with lament. If the church is the body of Christ, we have to confess that it was betrayed and crucified by its very members in Rwanda. The tragedy in Rwanda, however, was but a mirror reflecting the deep brokenness of the church worldwide.

How long, O God, will we go on with a mock Christianity that takes the tribalism of our world for granted?

How long, O God, will we be satisfied with the way things are?

How long, O God, will we try to "make some difference in the world" while leaving the basic patterns of the world unaffected?

How long, O God, will we take consolation in numbers, buildings, and structures, when millions of your children are dying?

How long, O Sovereign Lord, will we remain blind to the lessons of history?

Any resurrection of the church as the body of Christ must begin with lament, which is an honest look at the brokenness of the church. Without lament, we move on too quickly to reconstruction. Even as Rwamasirabo was narrating his story to us in the church building at Nyange, the new priest serving the church there only wanted to talk about the future. He told us how the parish was growing: six thousand new baptisms every year. He was excited and proud of his work in the parish. He even wanted money to build a new church!

But just as there is no resurrection without forgiveness, there is no hopeful resurrection that is not grounded in truthful memory, including the honest admission of failure. In the aftermath of Rwanda's genocide, we cannot just think in terms of more baptisms, newer churches, more missionaries, more schools, and so on. That became clear to me as I prayed at Nyange.

Nyange also made clear to me the role of anger in

resurrection. We all try as much as possible to hang onto what is in our lives, even when we know little good will come of it. Even when we know not much is working, we console ourselves anyway. We know that the way we have practiced our faith leaves much to be desired, but we look at the good it has been able to provide, and we think we are fine. Our dreams might be dead, but we hang onto their mummified skeletons because we are afraid of the unknown future.

But lament brings us to the breaking point. That is what the time of prayer around the altar pushed me to—a breaking point where I had to say, "I cannot take this any more!" I admit that I was afraid of the anger that welled up within me at that moment. I was unsettled by what I was thinking about the church as I prayed there. To be honest, I didn't know where it would lead. But then I realized that this righteous anger within me was a gift from God.

My anger at Nyange led me to see that the church in its current configuration is dead. The denominational church that is so grounded in racial, tribal, ethnic, and national identities is dead. Any church that thinks Hutu and Tutsi or black and white are natural does not have the life of Christ in it. The church that believes it is interesting or somehow advantageous to be American is the church of yesterday. That is the church that lies in the ruins at Nyange, with all the saints buried underneath crying, "How long?"

The resurrected church—the church of the future —must look and be different. It might more closely resemble our group of thirty-one people on pilgrimage: kneeling, joining hands, praying together above the altar. The resurrected church is drawn from different nations, black and white, African and Western, Hutu and Tutsi, Catholic, Protestant, and evangelical. It is a people on pilgrimage together—a mixed (and hopefully mixed-up) group, bearing witness to a new identity made possible by the gospel.

The mirror that is Rwanda brings us to a cry of lament on our knees. It brings us to the breaking point. Together we learn that we cannot take it anymore. We cannot go on in the same way.

But Rwanda also brings us to a place of hope. As I cried out on that altar at Nyange, "How long, O God?" I felt myself holding onto God more dearly than I had in years. I felt something of what Rwamasirabo was saying: "I do not believe in religion and priests, but I believe in God." Maybe the church is compromised. Maybe Christ's body is broken. But the longer I cried out to God, the more certain I was that Jesus is our only hope.

The resurrection of the church is in God's hands, and God is going to do it. I hear so much talk today about the reconstruction of Rwanda. Rwanda is in a building boom. Everywhere you go you'll find new homes, new supermarkets, new roads, and new airports. The government's 2020 Vision is to make Rwanda an African success story.

Churches and NGOs have joined this dream, from mission groups offering microfinance, telecommunications, and health care to church growth strategies employed in Kigali's new suburbs. For many people, it feels like an exciting time to be in Rwanda.

But I am disappointed that I do not hear much talk about the resurrection of the church. This may be because many Rwandans lost hope in the church after the genocide. Nyange reveals why. But what Nyange helped me to see in the ruins, skulls, and bones of that church building is that through the prayer of lament there is indeed hope for the church—but only *if* we can come to this breaking point of crying out together, "How long?"

After our visit to Nyange, we sat on an unusually quiet bus, making our way back to Kigali. We allowed the pain and tears of the story of Nyange to sink in. One of the pilgrims approached me and said that the text that came to her as we were praying at Nyange was Ezekiel 37. Right there on the bus, she and I read it together.

"Can these bones live?" the Lord asks the prophet as he stands overlooking a valley of dry bones (Ezekiel 37:3). Then the Lord commanded, "Prophesy to these bones ..." (v. 4). The Lord said to prophesy to the ruins. Then the Lord said to prophesy again. Finally, the text says, "And as I was prophesying, there was a noise, a rattling sound, and the bones came together, bone to bone" (v. 7).

I thought about what the text seemed to be saying—that even in the midst of what appears to be dead, God can issue a miracle of resurrection. The prophet is called to speak the words of this deep truth. But even while he is speaking them, a change begins to happen. What was dead is made alive again.

I thought about the signs of hope we had encountered on our pilgrimage. Just across the road from the church that was bulldozed at Nyange is the school where students had refused to separate Hutu from Tutsi in 1997. Most of them died together at the hands of the *interahamwe*, martyrs to the new identity that bound them together in life and in death.

But I also remembered Emmanuel Ulimubenshi and Niziyimana Emerthe, who lived through that massacre and formed a survivors' association. Together they visit schools, educating and inspiring other students in the virtue of courage. I thought of the Emmaus choir, composed of children of survivors and victims, now singing together songs of healing and hope. I thought of Josephine, who lost her entire family in the church at Cyangugu and nearly lost her own life but now heads a ministry of healing for World Vision in Rwanda.

As I remembered the stories of hope from that pilgrimage, I also thought of stories that I had read or encountered on my other visits to Rwanda. Giving thanks, my mind jumped from Father Andre Sibomana to Paul Rusesabagina to Carl Wilkens to Toni Locatelli to Sister Felicitee and others. In their stories I remembered the hope that is able to erupt in the face of death, betrayal, and madness.

That hope is what I want to leave you with — the hope that was possible even within the madness of genocide in Rwanda. But I don't want to remember these martyrs and courageous survivors as historic profiles in hope. I want to hold them up as examples of what is possible for us today. These stories point to a new Easter — a new resurrection that God can and does make possible in our time. For this Easter to become a reality in our time, it must be grounded in the following:

- **Memory** — as we take seriously the history of Rwanda and the tragic failure of the church to offer a baptism that ran deeper than tribalism
- **Mirror** — as we see in this story how resurrection happens in fresh interruptions of the so-called natural identities and patterns of life that we have assumed to be normal
- **Mission** — as we realize a new and urgent call to create and become the mixed-up people whose allegiance to our national, tribal, ethnic, or racial identities is suspect

We are called to be strange in the same way that the early Christian communities were strange to the world around them. The community in Antioch brought together Jews and Samaritans, Greeks and Romans, slaves and free, men and women in a way that was so confusing that people around them didn't know what to call them. So they called them "Christians." The only way they knew how to describe their peculiar actions was to say that they were followers of an odd preacher from Galilee.

The world is longing for such new and odd communities in our time. Rwanda brings the church to the breaking point and reveals that the time for such a fresh eruption of Christian community and identity is long overdue. I pray the time is now and that the resurrection might begin in us.

Notes

Chapter 1: An Easter Season of Bodies

1. Dietrich Bonhoeffer, as quoted in Marva J. Dawn, *Powers, Weakness, and the Tabernacling of God* (Grand Rapids: Eerdmans, 2001), 5.
2. Quoted in Peter Hebblethwaite, "In Rwanda, 'Blood Is Thicker Than Water,'" *National Catholic Reporter* (June 3, 1994).

Chapter 2: What Happened

1. Personal account taken from Andre Sibomana, Alison Des Forges, and Carina Tertsakian, *Hope for Rwanda: Conversations with Laure Guilbert and Herve Deguine* (London: Pluto Press, 1999), 62.
2. My thematic account of Rwanda's genocide highlights the lessons I want to draw from this tragedy. For a detailed historical account, see Gérard Prunier, *The Rwandan Crisis: History of a Genocide* (New York: Columbia University Press, 1995).
3. Javan Sebasore in John Ruchyahana, *The Bishop of Rwanda: Finding Forgiveness amidst a Pile of Bones* (Nashville: Nelson, 2007), 88.

4. Adalbert in Jean Hatzfeld, *Machete Season: The Killers in Rwanda Speak* (New York: Farrar, Straus & Giroux, 2005), 140.

5. Philip Gourevitch, *We Wish to Inform You That Tomorrow We Will Be Killed with Our Families* (New York: Farrar, Straus & Giroux, 1998), 136.

6. General Dallaire's account can been seen in the Steven Silver documentary film *The Last Just Man* (Canada, 2001).

7. Gourevitch, *We Wish to Inform You*, 153.

8. General Dallaire in Ruchyahana, *Bishop of Rwanda*, 82.

9. Gourevitch, *We Wish to Inform You*, 170–71.

10. Hatzfeld, *Machete Season*, 122–23.

Chapter 3: The Story That Made Rwanda

1. John Hanning Speke, *Journal of the Discovery of the Source of the Nile* (Eugene, Ore.: Wipf and Stock, 2007), xvii.

2. The children of Ham, who did not cover his father's nakedness when he found him drunk in his tent, were cursed by their grandfather in Genesis 9:25: "Cursed be Canaan! The lowest of slaves will he be to his brothers." White Europeans in the modern era reasoned that these sons of Ham had migrated to Africa and were still under the curse of Noah. Thus, the enslavement of black Africans had a "biblical" justification. This misreading of Scripture persisted into the late twentieth century in many churches of the American South.

3. Speke, *Journal*, 241.

4. Beyond the similarities of physical features, Speke believed that the genealogy of superior African peoples could be traced back to Semitic roots. "The traditions of the imperial government of Abyssinia go as far back as the Scriptural age of King David," he wrote, "from whom the late reigning king of Abyssinia, Sahela Selassie, traced his descent." Speke, *Journal*, 241.

Chapter 4: The Stories That Form Us

1. Thomas Hobbes, *Leviathan*, I:13.
2. According to UNICEF, 9.7 million children under 5 died in 2007 from all causes—that works out to 26,000 per day. An estimated 53% of these deaths were caused by hunger—which works out to 14,000 per day.

Chapter 5: Postures of Christian Social Engagement

1. John Perkins, lecture, Duke Divinity School Center for Reconciliation, Teaching Communities Week (2007).

Chapter 6: Interruptions

1. Sibomana et al., *Hope for Rwanda*, 68.
2. Sibomana et al., *Hope for Rwanda*, 67.

Chapter 7: Making a Prophetic Posture Possible

1. Wilkens tells his story in the PBS Frontline documentary *Ghosts of Rwanda*, distributed by Paramount Home Entertainment (2004), approximately 120 minutes.
2. Sibomana et al., *Hope for Rwanda*, 130.
3. Sibomana et al., *Hope for Rwanda*, 132.
4. Michel deCerteau, *The Practice of Everyday Life* (Berkeley: University of California Press, 1988), 35–37.
5. Personal notes from visit to the school (December 21, 2004).
6. Mahmoud Mamdani, *When Victims Become Killers* (Princeton, N.J.: Princeton University Press, 2001), 226.
7. Martin Luther King Jr., "Letter from a Birmingham Jail" in Clayborne Carson, ed., *The Autobiography of Martin Luther King Jr.* (New York: Warner Books, 1998), 191–92.

Acknowledgments

I HAVE DEDICATED THIS BOOK TO MY MOTHER, MAGDALENE, because all I have tried to do here is to put into words what she lives out. She has taught me what it means to be a Christian, even without using so many words. Her joyous seriousness about life, God, and the church, as well as her determination to keep going in the face of life's challenges, are lessons that I will ever cherish. Since my father died in 1972, she has worked tirelessly to raise seven children, send us to school, and keep us out of trouble. In this way she continues to model for me the tenderness of care as well as the virtues of hope and courage. Even though she has lived in Uganda for well over sixty years, she still speaks Luganda with an accent—which has led me to understand the Christian challenge in our time as one of learning to speak with an accent. In a way that is all that this book is about.

For the last six years I have taught and worked at Duke Divinity School. I am grateful to Dean Greg

Jones and the faculty of the Duke Divinity School for taking the risk of inviting and welcoming an African Catholic priest in their midst. Working in such a denominationally diverse and theologically rich context has been one of the greatest gifts I could ever ask for.

Having the honor and privilege to serve as a founding co-director of the Duke Center for Reconciliation (*http://www.divinity.duke.edu/reconciliation/index.html*) has been another gift, which has led me on many journeys and offered me wonderful opportunities to see signs of God's new creation even in unexpected places. I am particularly grateful to my friend and co-director, Chris Rice, and others with whom I share this journey and work at the center. In our book *Reconciling All Things*, the first in a series of books published by Duke Center for Reconciliation in partnership with InterVarsity Press, Chris and I share our journey and the key convictions that sustain our work at the center as we pursue God's mission of reconciliation in a broken world.

It is the desire to understand, pursue, and live out a vision of God's new creation amidst the scandalous divisions of tribalism in its many forms that drives my work at the intersection of being a teacher, scholar, priest, and the co-director of a Center for Reconciliation. I seek concrete signs of this new creation not only in Africa but throughout the world.

I am so glad that in this quest I am not alone but

that I continue to discover and receive the gifts of wonderful friends and companions like Jonathan Wilson-Hartgrove. Jonathan is one of those visionary and dedicated people who not only knows what needs to be done but also how to get it done. He encouraged me to write this book, and then he offered to help me write it. I am deeply grateful to Jonathan. Without him this book would probably not have been written, certainly not in such a fresh and timely fashion.

And finally, I am grateful to my editors at Zondervan for the grace and patience they have shown in working with us, and for the care and dedication with which they have attended to this book. Thank you, Angela Scheff, Bob Hudson, and everyone else on the team at Zondervan.

EMMANUEL KATONGOLE
Pentecost 2008